Kathy,
From your Friends at the
Capital Hotel. Enjoy the book.

A CAPITAL IDEA

Jimmy Moulton

Lilian Matzgranian

Carolyn Zaleswski

Karen Moser

Angie Gathi

A Capital Idea

An
Illustrated
History
of the
Capital
Hotel

Steven B. Weintz

The University of Arkansas Press
Fayetteville
2002

06   05   04   03   02   5   4   3   2   1

Designed by Liz Lester

LIBRARY OF CONGRESS CATALOGING-IN-PUBLICATION DATA

Weintz, Steven B.
    A capital idea : an illustrated history of the Capital
Hotel / Steven B. Weintz.
        p.   cm.
    ISBN 1-55728-727-9 (cloth)
    1. Capital Hotel (Little Rock, Ark.) 2. Hotels—
Arkansas—Little Rock--History. I. Title.

TX941.C35 W45 2002
647.94767'7301—dc21

                                                    2002005679

Frontispiece: The Capital Hotel, 2002, with the Stephens building in the background. *(Photo by Janet Warlick, Camera Work)*

Jackson T. Stephens.
(Photo courtesy Stephens, Inc.)

DEDICATION

This book is dedicated to Jackson T. Stephens.
Because of his business and personal interests, support,
and generosity, the Capital Hotel not only has a history,
but a present and future as well.

"If it were not for the Stephens family, this hotel would be a dilapidated old building. But because of their faith in the people of this state, they have turned it into a living piece of history for everyone to enjoy."

Joe B. Rantisi, General Manager
The Capital Hotel
March, 2001

CONTENTS

Heavy brass shoeshine pedestals from the barber shop of the Capital Hotel circa 1908. The pedestals were bought by Parker Westbrook in the mid-1970s at an auction to sell off many of the hotel artifacts. Westbrook attended the auction with then governor David Pryor for whom he served as special assistant. Prior to his position with Pryor, Westbrook also served in the same capacity for Sen. J. William Fulbright who ran his 1944 and 1962 campaigns from the Capital Hotel. *(Courtesy of Parker Westbrook. Photo by Janet Warlick, Camera Work)*

ACKNOWLEDGMENTS

To Bill Worthen, director of the Historic Arkansas Museum, who took time to read and comment on the first draft of this manuscript.

And to the Cromwell Firm, and especially to Margaret Hatchett, who provided many of the photographs, facts, files, and vital information to make this book a success.

Thanks also to Andrea Cassinelli, Guner Eruren, Scott Ford, Jim Pfeifer, Watt Gregory, Gene Levy, Larry Martin, Scott Martin, Joe Rantisi, Doyle Rogers, Kent Taylor, and Parker Westbrook for taking the time to share their experiences relating to the Capital Hotel.

With thanks to Frank Fellone, Barry Arthur, and the *Arkansas Democrat-Gazette* for permission to reprint articles and photographs relating to the Capital.

To Larry Malley and the staff at the University of Arkansas Press for their professional assistance in copy editing, book design and print production, and marketing.

Jackson T. "Steve" Stephens Jr.
*(Photo by Janet Warlick,
Camera Work)*

With thanks and gratitude to Jackson T. "Steve" Stephens Jr., who initiated this project and provided funding for the research and writing of this book.

Introduction

Writing a book is a little like painting.

You can set five artists up in front of a subject—the same subject—and you'll get five totally different paintings.

So it is with writing.

In considering the approach to this book, there were a number of different angles I could have chosen, covering a variety of interests and disciplines: history, architecture, politics, business, and people. Actually the history of the Capital Hotel has *all* of these ingredients.

But first and foremost I am of the belief that books need to be entertaining, not merely a black-and-white vehicle to communicate data and information, which I believe we have too much of in today's world.

Certainly I had some fun researching and writing this book. Hotels make interesting backdrops for all sorts of stories.

Joe Rantisi, the current general manager of the Capital told me, "People do a lot of strange things in hotels. Sometimes they do things in hotels they would normally not do where they live, because everyone knows them at home."

Mr. Rantisi's comment reminds me of the soap-opera-grade mini-series *Hotel* that ran back in the '80s during the days when the TV series *Dallas* was so popular. From the one or two episodes that I am embarrassed to admit I watched, I remember that the basic theme was that "anything can happen in a hotel." People are married, born, and die. In the privacy of hotel rooms, people argue, laugh, make love, do business, lobby, and legislate.

The Capital Hotel is currently celebrating its 125th anniversary. Over this period of history, undoubtedly every form of human behavior and activity has been expressed (if not recorded) within its walls.

To further illustrate his point, Mr. Rantisi told me a story about one of his guests. "We had this customer who was so very rude. He was yelling at everyone and not satisfied with anything! His behavior was so bad I finally had to talk to him. I told him that we appreciated his business, but that we didn't need it to the point of allowing him to belittle the staff. I told him I would be happy to make other arrangements at another hotel. Our guest said he didn't realize that he was being so rude and actually thanked me! On the fourth day of his stay, he called me up at the front desk and said, 'I want you to come up to my room, *I want to surrender myself to you!*' I said, 'What?' He said, 'Call the FBI. I am not coming out by myself . . . Please would you come to my room?' So I called the guest services manager, Ronnie Jackson, and said we had a guest who wanted to 'surrender.' It turns out that he had allegedly embezzled about a *billion* dollars. He was very emotional, and grateful to me. He asked if I would ship his personal items to his sister at the address he gave me. 'Here is my attorney's name. Please call him for me . . . and here are my credit cards. Let's settle my account.' So, I called the FBI, they showed up, and he surrendered to them. It was pretty wild."

So in addition to writing about history, architecture, politics, business, and people, I've tried to capture a few of these sorts of stories for no other purpose than they are fun and entertaining. There is nothing worse than a boring book.

IN MEMORIAM

Ed Cromwell.
(Photo by Andrew Kilgore)

EDWIN BOYKIN CROMWELL
NOVEMBER 13, 1909–SEPTEMBER 22, 2001

By all accounts, Ed Cromwell was considered to be the founding father of historic preservation in Arkansas. His September 23, 2001, obituary in the *Arkansas Democrat-Gazette* noted, "He had a fierce commitment to protecting Little Rock's historical treasures and advocated preservation at a time in the 1960s and 1970s when a majority of people favored urban renewal strategies that demolished inner cities for the sake of new development."

It was Cromwell's vision that resulted in Little Rock's first convention center: a complex of buildings including the Camelot Hotel, the Arkansas Bar Center, a restored Robinson Auditorium, and Public Plaza—all on the Arkansas River. At the same time, Cromwell began buying up and restoring old homes around MacArthur Park; this work eventually led to the creation by others of the Quapaw Quarter Historic District. For twenty-five years, Cromwell served as chairman of the Arkansas Territorial Restoration, now the Arkansas Historic Museum. But of all his many career accomplishments, Cromwell is best known—and was most proud of—his relentless work to save the Capital Hotel.

For nine months prior to his death, I worked with Ed Cromwell on this book. As we poured over boxes of notes, design sketches, and engineering project manuals, I witnessed his "indefatigable resolve" balanced with a gentleness and kindness of spirit that made Ed truly a remarkable human being. He was a true southern gentleman.

It was indeed a privilege to work with Ed on a personal level and to put down on paper his story and the story of the Capital Hotel. Cromwell "sought to preserve those historic buildings that distinguish Little Rock and, in so doing, helped residents remember their own past."

This book tells the story of, and pays tribute to, a great and gentle man and the historic old hotel that he loved so dearly.

NED SHANK
February 19, 1956–November 30, 2000

I never met Ned Shank, a talented, gifted preservationist, artist, and writer.

Ned was killed in a terrible bicycle accident on November 30, 2000, almost a year before I began work on this book.

In 1979 Ed Cromwell commissioned Ned to conduct historical research prior to the restoration of the Capital Hotel. The factual information and details that Ned discovered amid hundreds of musty, yellowed pages of old newspapers and city directories gave Cromwell and his restoration crew invaluable clues about the original building structure.

Ed and Ned held each other in high personal and professional esteem. They were friends. It is both sad yet just that they now share this tribute which punctuates their work on the Capital Hotel.

I have come to know Ned—both through his historical research and from talks with his wife of twenty-three years: the writer and poet, Crescent Dragonwagon, co-founder with Ned of the Writers' Colony at Dairy Hollow in Eureka Springs.

In a collection of writings and illustrations, *With and Without Ned,* about her late husband, Crescent says, "Stories, not buildings themselves, and what they said about people, were at the heart of his preservationism. Although he could talk technically with the best of them (and frequently beat me at Scrabble using obscure architectural words, such as 'quoin' or 'lintel'), to Ned, preservation's connective tissue was not building material but people and human history: personal and societal."

Ned's research on the Capital covered the era between 1872 and 1908. Ned's revised and condensed narrative is contained in the first chapter of this book and gives valuable insight about the history of the Capital Hotel today.

With deep gratitude and appreciation . . . thank you Ned Shank.

Ned Shank.
(Photo by Andrew Kilgore)

A Capital Idea

CHAPTER ONE

THE EARLY HISTORY
OF THE
CAPITAL HOTEL,
1872 TO 1908

The history of the Capital Hotel begins in 1872 with a carpetbagger named Denckla and a highly esteemed lawyer and judge who had an open mind to a project that might encourage economic development in downtown Little Rock.

It was a different world. It was an era later to be known as Reconstruction. The Civil War had ended. Railroads were being built north and south, east and west. Roads were still mostly unpaved. Indoor plumbing and electric lights were soon to become astounding modern marvels of technology. The economy was booming. It was a time when opportunistic Yankees invaded the southern homelands in search of making a fast dollar.

Little Rock ("la petite roche") had been christened in 1722 by the French explorer Bernard de la Harpe, who sailed up the Arkansas River and anchored in deep water, surrounded by magnificent rock bluffs. La Harpe established a trading outpost that became a port and point of commerce, its proximity to the river being an all-important fact in its commercial development, much like other river cities of the time: Memphis, St. Louis, and Vicksburg, to name just a few. Little Rock's growth started slowly. In 1865 the population was estimated at four thousand. But by 1900 it was forty thousand. After the Civil War, the railroads started to be built, thus providing Little Rock with a stronger link to the outside world and urban centers like Saint Louis, Chicago, and New York. Arkansas timber, apples, and other agricultural produce could be shipped out of state. Still, local commerce was uncommercialized by twentieth-century standards. Business was conducted in small shops on a personal basis. Shop owners ordered their wares wholesale from traveling salesmen. It was an era of patent medicines and miracle cures.

Representative of such heavily promoted patent medicines was Dr. A. Q. Simmon's "Genuine Vegetable Liver Medicine . . . For all diseases of the liver including sourness of the stomach, loss of appetite, dyspepsia, sick headache, costiveness, etc." This advertising copy appeared repeatedly in the *Arkansas Gazette* in the late 1870s in a tombstone ad. Underneath a line drawing of Dr. A. Q.—who wore flowing white hair, beard, and a solemn expression befitting one who has struggled and conquered liver disease—was a testimonial by Arthur Left, minister of the Methodist Episcopal Church South and Grand S. Warden of Grand Lodge, Georgia, who proclaimed unequivocally that Dr. A. Q. Simmon's medicine had "saved my life, and from my knowledge of its use in Georgia it has produced more permanent cures in Liver Diseases than any or all others combined" (*Arkansas Gazette,* December 15, 1876).

The transient traveling salesmen and barge and rail crews who worked or passed through Little Rock were sometimes an uncivilized lot—ideal clients for Kate Merrick "queen of the dell," a notorious madam who ran a brothel amidst the seedy taverns on the east side of the north edge of Little Rock also known as Fighting Alley, Battle Row, and Hell's Half Acre (Jim Lester and Judy Lester. *Greater Little Rock.* Norfolk, Va.: Donning, 1986).

Aside from rail workers and salesmen, there was a new breed of Yankee businessman who came to town. One of these was William P. Denckla, a railroad tycoon from New York. Denckla had money, and his wealth and reputation enabled him to make some notable alliances in Arkansas, one of which was Arkansas Supreme Court justice George C. Watkins.

A Place to Do Business

William P. Denckla wasn't interested in building a hotel. Little Rock already had a hotel, and a very nice one at that: the Metropolitan. What was needed was someplace to do business. A place that could house a variety of small shops, professional offices, and apartments for traveling salesmen: "bachelor quarters."

> The building, which has been known as the Capital Hotel for so many years, was not originally built as a hotel. The ground on which the building stands belonged originally to Judge George C. Watkins, former chief justice of the Supreme Court of Arkansas. He sold the property to W. P. Denckla of New York, one of the builders of the Little Rock and Fort Smith Railroads. In 1870 Denckla erected a building which was intended to be used for stores and offices. The building when erected was three stories in height. Later a fourth story was added and still later, only a few years ago, an addition was built on the rear of the building.
>
> (*Arkansas Gazette,* July 25, 1908)

> The history of a building is always the sum total of the small and large parts its creators, builders and users have made over the years of its existence. The Capital Hotel began its life as a three-story, rapidly constructed commercial and speculative venture by a non-native capitalist during a time of exuberant economic expansion in Little Rock. The land the building stood on, recently settled and controlled by white settlers, belonged to a well-established Little Rock man, whose family eventually came to own the building itself. The Watkins family saw the building through its early years until the turn of the century, through its change into a hotel, through its expansions and additions, and through numerous of its tenants.
>
> (*Arkansas Gazette,* August 15, 1908)

> The new block of buildings to be erected by Mr. Denckla opposite City Hall, will be the handsomest in the City. There will be six stores each three stories high, and the entire front of the block is to be iron and ornamental in character. The entire third floor will be arranged as sleeping arrangements for gentlemen, and is to be handsomely furnished and rented at reasonable rates.
>
> (*Arkansas Democrat,* December 14, 1881)

Construction of the Denckla Building

Actual construction of the Denckla building began in the spring of 1872 and continued on through the fall and winter and into the following spring. By the third week in November, in the *Gazette*'s last coverage of the building's progress in the year 1872, the work was far enough along for the paper to report that

> Just opposite City Hall the Denckla block is now approaching completion. The whole front is of iron, being the only block in the city with an all iron front. This block contains six stores, is three stories, and exceedingly handsome.
>
> (*Arkansas Gazette,* November 21, 1872)

The Cast-Iron Façade

Ned Shank, in his research notes on the Capital Hotel, which were completed in the early 1980s for architect Ed Cromwell, writes that "the classical, pleasingly repetitive arches and columns of the Denckla Block façade have been one of the building's lastingly interesting features."

The façades consist of prefabricated units made out of cast iron. Literally an assembled piecework of iron castings, the front of the building was designed, cast, and then shipped to the building site. A masonry building was constructed of the proper dimensions to receive the façade, which was then assembled and bolted onto the building as its walls went up. The façade was an integral structural element of the building, not just a cosmetic component.

Bill Worthen, director of the Historic Arkansas Museum in Little Rock, comments: "The structure (the Capital Hotel) has great importance in the history of architectural history of Arkansas. There are not that many structures still around from the early 1870s, certainly not of cast iron and of such a 'high' style . . ."

The façade on the Denckla Block bears no manufacturer's marks, although it is undoubtedly of American origin. Cast-iron façades are a uniquely American phenomenon, and there are numerous examples throughout the country including the entire California State Capitol in Sacramento, as well as the dome of the United States Capitol in Washington, D.C.

The origin of the cast-iron façade on the Denckla Block is somewhat unclear, with stories still circulating that it originated in Europe. A logical explanation appeared in the *Gazette* thirty-six years after the building's construction:

> It is said that the iron front of the building was constructed for A. T. Stewart, at one time the greatest merchant in New York City, and was to have been used in a new store building being erected by him in New York. For some reason the front was not accepted by Stewart and was purchased by the builder of the Capital Hotel.
>
> (*Arkansas Gazette,* July 25, 1908)

Since Denckla was from New York, we can conjecture that he must have made the business tie with Stewart and arranged for the shipment of the façade to Arkansas.

Cast-iron architecture has been described as the precursor of the American development of the modern skyscraper. Like modern skyscrapers, cast-iron buildings had components manufactured away from the building site; they were then rapidly assembled once delivered. This rapidity of construction can be seen in the building of the Denckla Block.

The Completion of Construction

The dozens of workers needed to construct a building of this size must have been kept busy throughout the winter of 1872. After the *Gazette*'s last news of the building in November, the newspaper reported in mid-January of the following year that "the windows [were] already in," and a coat of paint was sprucing up the looks of the building's cast-iron façade. The balance of the building's brick exterior was originally left unpainted. Additional exterior work in the form of a "thirteen feet wide plank sidewalk laid in front of the Denckla Block" was completed by the third week in February (*Arkansas Gazette,* February 12, 1873).

The Finished Appearance of the Building

The Denckla Block was an attractive building when completed. It stood three stories high, and its lightly colored decorative façade contrasted nicely with the plainer brick buildings on the street. The front of the building was painted, and various signs were placed directly on it. These first signs were attached flat against the building, rather than sticking them onto the shop windows on the ground floor. A remarkably clear stereoscopic photograph of the building taken during its first summer also shows the small advertising signs the shopkeepers placed in front of their businesses during the day on the Markham Street sidewalk as well as a large stuffed bear and a wooden Indian.

This photograph also shows that the brick wall facing the alley on the east side of the building was originally left unpainted. A tracery of iron fencing graced the top of the façade, and a classically inspired monogram, complete with broken pediment, crowned the building and served as the base for a flag pole. The monogram was probably constructed of sheet metal formed over a wood frame and was added to the building in mid-May of its first year (*Arkansas Gazette,* May 15, 1873).

The cast-iron façade of the Denckla Block is not merely a decorative veneer applied to another wall that actually holds up the building: it is in itself a structural wall, just as the exposed steel and concrete beams of modern architecture are actual structural components of their building.

So despite its traditional, classic appearance, the cast-iron façade of the Denckla Block represents a significant step by Americans toward modern architectural design. It was an exposed structural element, it was prefabricated away from and assembled at the building site, and it opened up a tremendous proportion of the exterior wall to windows.

The Purchase of the Denckla Building by the Watkins Heirs

Judge George C. Watkins died in 1872, just as the building was being completed. William Denckla's speculative interest in the property rings loud and clear because within only a few months after the building was completed, he sold the building to the Watkins heirs. Despite Watkins's death and the lengthy probating of his will, the Denckla building was immediately occupied. Judge Watkins's probate records (all 395 pages) provide excellent documentation on the building's early history and the cost of various improvements and repairs.

This remarkably clear stereoscopic photograph of the Denckla building was taken during its first summer. It shows the small advertising signs the shopkeepers placed in front of their businesses during the day on the Markham Street sidewalk as well as a large stuffed bear and a wooden Indian. *(Courtesy Arkansas History Commission)*

Shops, Offices, and Apartments

Modern urban planners have developed terms and concepts such as mixed-use development and three-dimensional zoning to promote a variety of activities in our urban areas to make them more vital and interesting. The ideas draw inspiration from what happened naturally in our cities in the late 1800s, and the Denckla Block serves as a good example of an early mixed-use development.

The newspaper reports of Denckla's construction plans announced that the building's three stories would be divided into three uses: shop space on the ground floor, offices on the second, and gentlemen's living quarters on the third (*Arkansas Gazette,* May 28, 1872). This plan was generally followed in the three years before the Capital Hotel's tenancy, although the third floor did accommodate some offices as well as apartments.

After the building opened, shopkeepers quickly moved in to the street-level shops. P. Raleigh was the first, opening a shop advertised as selling "Carpets and Furnishings Goods—Ladies, Gents and House" *(Little Rock City Directory, 1873–1874).* Raleigh occupied the middle rooms of the building, later to become the Capital Hotel lobby, with access to Markham Street provided by the rooms' two doors. Raleigh was followed ten days later by G. W. Lindley, who moved in next door, one door west towards Louisiana Street. The *Gazette* reported that Lindley's store "opened . . . for the sale of flowers, fruit and ornamental trees" (*Arkansas Gazette,* March 16, 1873). His listing in the city directory, however, advertised that he sold books and stationery, and served as a newsstand. Lindley shared his address with S. H. Timmons, who sold music and musical instruments *(Little Rock City Directory, 1873–1874).*

A third shop opened less than a month later, occupying the room on the corner of Louisiana and Markham Streets, the last available shop on the western half of the block. The *Gazette* reported on April 2, 1873, that the Burrows brothers

> . . . propose to do an extensive trade as Grocers and Tea dealers. Their stock of teas, coffees, etc. is large and choice . . . Their stock comprises, also, everything in the line of staples and fancy groceries. Housekeepers and country dealers will find it greatly to their advantage to make a trial of this firm. Purchases will be delivered without charge in any part of the city.

Returning to the eastern side of the Denckla Block, the two shops east of P. Raleigh's furnishings store were occupied by the merchants whose sidewalk advertising figures show up in the early stereoscopic photograph mentioned previously. Just east of the Raleigh store was Louis Ran's Tobacco, Cigar, Wine and Liquor Store. The wooden Indian pictured in the photograph stood in front of his shop, a traditional advertisement meaningful to all customers, some of whom could perhaps not read. The last store on the eastern side of the block, bordering on the alley, belonged to Morris and Withall, Furriers, Hats and Caps. Their stuffed bear, mounted on a small platform, standing upright on its rear legs and leaning on a tree limb, was an eye-catching and appropriate symbol for their business.

The upper stories housed a variety of occupants. The 1873 city directory shows a total of eleven of the forty-six rooms on the second and third floors occupied by a combination of attorneys, civil engineers, bridge builders, physicians, insurance and real estate agents, a broker, lumber dealer, and a mining engineer. Enough people had moved into the building by August that the *Gazette* reported:

> Howe, the painter, has placed a directory of the Denckla block at the front of the main stairs. It will contain the name of each lodger, his business and the number of the room he occupies. It is a thing long needed, and will be of great advantage to strangers.
>
> (*Arkansas Gazette,* August 16, 1873)

The third floor also housed gentlemen's apartments. The Watkins estate bought several sets of bedroom furniture for the building in 1875 and 1876, and various minor expenses for bedding and for laundering sheets for the furnished rooms also crop up irregularly in the Watkins probate records for this period of time before the Capital Hotel moved into the building.

The *Gazette* mentioned on September 7, 1876, that

> The Denckla block rooms have long been considered the most eligible quarters for bachelors that could be found in Little Rock, and for that reason they are seldom vacant. Being situated in the heart of the business portion of the city, in the finest block on the street, a residence in the Denckla has great attractions, and gentlemen in search of agreeable winter quarters will be delighted to learn that there are now in it a few rooms vacant and for rent.

From its opening in March 1873, then, until the end of 1876, the Denckla Block served as a mixed-use commercial building housing shops, offices, and men's apartments. During this three year period, the Watkins family operated and maintained the building along the lines of its original design.

The Brooks-Baxter War

Over its 125-year history, the Capital Hotel has had a long list of prominent lawmakers and politicians using the building as their campaign and official, or sometimes unofficial, legislative headquarters. In fact, no sooner had the Denckla building been constructed than it was in the midst of a "unique war," recounted in detail by Hampton Roy (*Arkansas Gazette,* February 28, 1984). A century before the dimpled-chad controversy in Florida in the Bush-Gore election, Arkansas was the scene of a contested political victory that ended in significant bloodshed: the so-called Brooks-Baxter War. Following the inauguration of Elisha Baxter on January 6, 1873, "About a dozen armed men hurried to the governor's office in the statehouse, which still stands across from the Capital Hotel, and physically expelled Baxter from his office. Baxter set up his headquarters at the Anthony House, then a hotel two blocks east of the capital . . . In the following month, there were four bloody skirmishes, one of them in front of the Capital Hotel (Denckla building). About 200 men were killed or were wounded . . . the crisis sharply divided the state."

President Grant actually had to step in and settle the political controversy, and the Denckla building had its first taste of Arkansas politics.

The Birth of the Capital Hotel

"Christmas Is Coming" proclaimed the advertising headline for Kellog & Company, a retail shop located in the Denckla Block. It was just ten days before Christmas and the December 15 edition of the *Arkansas Gazette* carried many holiday ads including the copy for Kellog and Company:

> Everybody will expect a present of some kind from a relative or friend. In view of this we have purchased a very large and well-assorted stock of goods especially adapted to the occasion. Ladies' work boxes, writing desks, ladies' and gents' dressing cases. Pearl and shell card cases, money books, gold pens. Cribbage boards and boxes. Chessmen, dominoes and several pretty new games never before introduced into this city . . . Last but not least, we have several handsome pianos and organs of every best manufacture at prices and on terms never before offered in this city. Do not wait until the last day to buy your presents, but come now and make your selections while you may have a choice.

Other merchants proclaimed availability of wares suitable for Christmas gifts. "A world of thanks is due to the botanist who first discovered the virtues of Quillaya Saponaria, or Soap Tree of Chili. The wonderful cleansing and purifying property of its bark gives to the fragrant Sozodont much of its unrivalled efficacy as a preservative of teeth."

Miller and Penzel liquor store announced that they had a supply of T & J. W. Gaff straight Bourbon whiskies for sale. The ever-popular steamed oysters were again available at Monrey's eating establishment. And finally "Fifty thousand shingles" were for sale "very low" by M. Hickey, who could be found at "the corner of Rector Avenue and Ninth Street."

Amidst the holiday cheer, a somber headline on December, 15, 1876, brought tragic news to *Arkansas Gazette* readers:

Fearful Fire!
Little Rock Receives Another Visit from the Devouring and Consuming Element.

> The Magnificent Metropolitan Hotel with All the Buildings on the West to City Hall Burned to the Ground. Loss Estimated at Fully $150,000, with Insurance at Less than One-Sixth the Amount. Only by the Heroic Efforts of the Fire Department that the Flames were Prevented from Sweeping Main Street.

A fire of this proportion was a huge disaster, perhaps exacerbated by the lack of city cisterns, poor fire water pumping machines and rotten hoses as charged by the *Gazette*. The fire was witnessed by "nearly the entire population of the city" from its start the night of Thursday, December 14:

> "About 9 o'clock last night a fire alarm was sounded. Simultaneously with the sounds, flames were discovered breaking out of the roof of the City icehouse, at the foot of Main Street, and in the rear of the old Commercial

house which formed a part of the Metropolitan Hotel. The ice house was composed entirely of wood, and was soon burned to the ground . . ."

(*Arkansas Gazette,* December 15, 1876)

The buildings it destroyed occupied an entire block in the heart of downtown Little Rock on the north, or the Arkansas River side, of West Markham Street between Main Street on the east and Louisiana Street on the west. The State Capitol itself was only two blocks to the west. The building that would soon become the Capital Hotel was just across the street.

With its windows no doubt alive with light, reflecting the flames of the fire only one hundred feet away, the future Capital Hotel building survived the fire unscathed, surviving perhaps in part due to the efforts of John Baskins and others, who were paid the day following the fire a total of $1.75 for "Services to building as watchmen during the fire in the night of the 14th instant" (*Arkansas Gazette,* December 16, 1876).

Among those buildings which were destroyed were the Dodge Block, "Worth about $20,000, and the . . . most profitable property in the city as regards the question of rent-income," and the Metropolitan Hotel, "valued at about $45,000" and "bringing a good rental" (*Arkansas Gazette,* December 15, 1876).

Little Rock was now without a hotel—a fact much lamented by the *Gazette* in the week following the disaster. "We suppose that the Metropolitan Hotel, its business and associations, has been missed greater than any other establishment it has ever been the misfortune of Little Rock to lose" (*Arkansas Gazette,* December 21, 1876).

A week after the fire, the *Gazette* was able to go on to report the happy news that a new hotel was to be started up. The headline of that article: "A Hotel at Last." The "Fearful Fire" reported by the *Gazette,* blazing across the street on the night of December 14, 1876, set in motion a rapid series of events that would permanently change the identity, character, and use of the Denckla Block.

The Capital Hotel, 1876 to 1884

When the Metropolitan Hotel burned to the ground, a block away from the Denckla Block on that mid-December night in 1876, the Metropolitan Hotel's manager, Col. A. G. DeShon wasted little time in securing new quarters for reestablishing a hotel.

The *Gazette* was able to report merely seven days after the fire that DeShon, who would run the new hotel until his death seven years later, had secured the Denckla Block in which to reopen his hotel. The newspaper described the sequence of events in an article heavily laced with expressions of local patriotism and closing with a not-too-subtle bid to name the new hotel:

A Hotel at Last
The Stately Denckla Block to Be Converted into a First-Class Public House.

Every citizen has recognized the necessity of having a good hotel in this, the state capital, and the question naturally arose as to how such an end could be attained. It was an impossibility to build in time for the meeting of the legislature, and the immediate necessities of the city in this particular were becoming more apparent every day, as our city is at present quite full of travelers, who complain that they cannot receive proper accommodations, and in leaving naturally carrying with them a bad reputation of Little Rock and the enterprise of her citizens.

But Col. DeShon, the efficient manager of the late Metropolitan, was equal to the occasion, and in casting about for another location to establish a first-class hotel, his choice naturally fell upon the handsome Denckla block, the prettiest and most commodious building in the city, located on the corner of Markham and Louisiana streets.

Mr. W. F. Wright, the agent having the block in charge, was approached on the subject, but at first he was not inclined to enter into the arrangement. The block was rented in a very profitable way and to good and select tenants, with whom Mr. Wright was loth to part. The great needs of the city were brought to bear in the matter, however, and only yesterday Mr. Wright reluctantly consented to lease the block to Messrs. Adams and DeShon for hotel purposes. Nothing but the absolute business requirements of the city would have induced him to take this step, and in a note to his tenants he says:

I feel called upon to say that I part with you with regret, and only the peculiar circumstances surrounding us prompts me to make the move. But in view of the urgent necessity that our city, just now struggling into life and stability, should have a public house for the accommodations of the traveling community, and the peculiar fitness of the building and site, and advantages to the owners, all warrant and demand the change.

So far as we have learned, the tenants of the building have acquiesced to the request, with a cheerfulness that deserved commendation. Many of them have occupied their rooms until they appear to their eyes like a home, while a number of attorneys occupy good and advantageous offices, and the lower floors as business stands are equal to any in the city. So when we see citizens thus willingly vacating premises that are in every way advantageous to them, we feel as though public spirit is not yet dead among our people, and that a city is bound to success when her citizens show such a readiness to sacrifice their private interests for the public good.

So far as we have yet learned in reference to the plans of the new lessee, the management of the hotel will be entirely under the control of Col. DeShon. The rooms occupied by Mr. Hyde as a hat and clothing store will be converted into an office. The portion of the building known as the Surprise Store, will be used as a dining hall. We have not been informed as to what disposition is to be made of the other store-rooms on the front floor, but as the hotel is to have all the necessary attachments required by a first-class establishment, such as billiard hall, bar, barber-shop, etc., it is probable that the space will be occupied in a useful and appropriate manner. The Denckla at present contains forty-six rooms, eighteen of which are large enough to be converted into two rooms each, giving it sixty-four rooms in all. It is the intention of the new management, however, to build an additional wing on the Shell alley and on the Louisiana street front to run back sixty feet, which will give about fifty more rooms, enabling the house to accommodate fully 200 guests or over at one time.

But as the Denckla now stands, without addition or alteration, it is by far the handsomest and most commodious building ever yet used in this city for hotel purposes, and we congratulate the lessees upon their good luck in being able to secure it.

The hotel will be furnished in a first-class manner throughout, the management hoping to be able to commence operations the first week in January. We have not learned what name Col. DeShon has chosen for his Phoenix, but under any name we wish it a hearty success.

(Arkansas Gazette, December 21 1876)

The *Gazette* later reported, on December 27, on the naming of the hotel:

Privilege of Giving a Name to the New Hotel Delegated to a Lady.

In casting about for a name for their new hotel to be located in the Denckla building, Messrs. Adams and DeShon happily hit upon the expedient of submitting the whole matter to the very good taste of a lady, and the following note, which explains itself, was received in reply to their courteous request:

Little Rock, Dec. 26 Major John D. Adams:

Appreciating the compliment of being asked to name your hotel, I can think of no name more appropriate than "Capital Hotel," as it is a capital enterprise located in a capital building, which will do honor to the capital of the state, and I trust prove a capital success to yourself and Major DeShon. Respectfully, your friend, Mrs. Morehead Wright

And as the "Capital Hotel" it will be known

The Conversion of the Denckla Building

A great deal of work needed to be done before the hotel could open the following month, and DeShon must have gone about his tasks with determination. Having settled the name of the business, DeShon headed north to St. Louis to purchase "a full outfit of first-class furniture for the new Capital Hotel."

Meanwhile, the Watkins heirs were having the building prepared for the Capital Hotel's imminent occupancy. As mentioned in the *Gazette* article, the previous tenants of the second and third story offices and rooms were evicted.

The single biggest expense in preparing for the Capital Hotel's occupancy was for "calsomining and painting in all the rooms and halls in the Denckla Block and calsomining the Store and offices." The total cost of this task was $655. Judging from the expenses listed in the probate records, the Denckla Block and the Capital Hotel received many applications of calcimine, also spelled "Kalsomine" or "calsomine." Calcimine is a kind of whitewash, used particularly on plaster walls. It is made by mixing up water, glue, any desired tints, and a substance called whiting, which is composed of finely ground and washed calcium carbonate derived from plant ashes, bones, or shells. Calcimine would have been used to freshen and color the plaster

Drawing of the newly con-
verted Denckla building: the
New Capital Hotel. *(Courtesy
Arkansas History Commission)*

wall surfaces in the Capital Hotel, with the more expensive oil-based paint being
reserved for use on the wooden trim and other less-expansive areas needing a decorative or protective coat of colored paint.

By the third week of January, DeShon had returned from his furniture
purchasing expedition to St. Louis, the building preparations were completed, and
the new furnishings had been installed. On the eve of the Capital Hotel's official
opening on January 21, 1877, the *Gazette* ran a long article describing the new
business, quoted below in its full and comprehensive detail:

Capital Hotel
The Finest Building in the South
Used for Hotel Purposes

The Capital Hotel opens for the reception of guests and the accommo-
dation of the general public tomorrow. As all know, it is located in the
Denckla block, which was originally built with a view to being converted

into a hotel, therefore its adaptability to its present use is quite natural. The Denckla is, without a doubt, one of the finest edifices in the south, constructed in the most modern style, and fairly rivals some of the many buildings of which the Garden City of Chicago is so proud. The exterior is grand, and Col. DeShon, the managing lessee, has so fitted up the interior in the very best style known to the upholsterer, that it is in keeping with the stately appearance of the establishment. The entrance is on Markham Street, the general entrance being on each side of the stairway, which forms the ladies' entrance, and leads to a magnificently furnished room on the second floor. On the first floor is the office, connected with which are all accommodations found in modern hotels, which in an adjoining room, easy of access by side doors, is the restaurant, which is, we believe, under the proprietorship of Mr. Frank Mourey, who has an excellent reputation in that line.

The second and third floors are to be occupied as rooms, there now being accommodations for about eighty guests. These rooms are furnished in a style never before seen in Little Rock or any other southern city, giving quarters generally equal in comfort and surroundings to those furnished by the Southern Hotel of St. Louis, or the Palmer House of Chicago. Every room is handsomely carpeted, generally with superior English-body Brussels, containing in the pattern such daintily contrived figures that it looks as though it were a pity to walk on them. The furniture is grand and massive, the bridal chamber looking as gorgeous as a mind-picture created by the dreamy stories of the Arabian Nights. The building is lighted with gas throughout. Every arrangement is made for prompt attendance to the wants of occupants of rooms, there being in the office a handsomely framed machine known as a patent magnetic annunciator with figures representing the numbers of rooms; by pressing an ornamental little knob sunk into the side of any room, the annunciator being connected with the room in question by a magnetic wire, immediately indicates with clock-like-hand pointing at the number, the room in which service is desired.

The rooms of the hotel are all large, light and comfortable, the corridors and stairways broad, and there are no intricate passages to confuse or mislead strangers to the building who may be attempting to escape in case of a fire.

Little Rock has in the Capital hotel, an establishment of which her citizens may well be proud, and which travelers who may rest therein will always speak of in the highest terms for come from where they may they cannot help being satisfied with and favorably impressed by this superb establishment.

The magnificent carpets which adorn the floors of the Capital were furnished by the well known carpet-house of Messrs. C. L. Bray & Co., North Fourth Street, St. Louis, and are wonderful and handsome productions of the loom. The furniture which so tastily adorns the rooms was purchased from the firm of Messrs. Burrell & Comstock, of the same city.

Messrs. Adams & DeShon are the lessees, but the hotel will be under the exclusive management of Col. DeShon, while Col. James A. Henry and Mr. Ed Small will be found in the office.

Ten days later the Capital Hotel's sign went up, mounted against the building above the entrance. On January 31, 1877, the *Gazette* reported "the Capital Hotel has put up a gilt sign, which is very appropriate for a first-class, gilt-edged hotel."

An Addition to the Building

The occupancy of the Denckla Block by the Capital Hotel prompted a significant number of physical alterations and additions to the original building during the first few years of the hotel's residency. The most significant change occurred the first year with the addition of a three-story brick wing with ground-floor shop space and two stories of guest rooms made to the rear of the main building.

The day of the hotel's opening, architect J. G. Steacy published a solicitation for construction bids for the addition. Architect Steacy must have been engaged shortly after the lessees secured the building in December to have had the plans ready immediately after the opening a month later.

The ad ran as follows:

Proposals
TENDERS
For the Erection and Completion
Of
TWO WINGS TO THE CAPITAL HOTEL
Each 45 x 60 will be received by the
Undersigned until March 10th. The lowest
Or any tender not necessarily accepted.
J.G. STEACY, Architect.

(*Arkansas Gazette,* February 22, 1887)

This advertisement for two wings indicates that Adams, a business associate of DeShon's, and DeShon planned a major expansion of their facility. Work began a full five months later, although the expansion plans were reduced, and only one of the two wings was built.

The *Gazette* reported on June 28, that work was beginning on the hotel's addition: "The sheds in the rear of the Capital Hotel are being removed and work will at once be commenced on the addition to be built to the main hotel building."

A frame house that stood on the lot was moved down to 10th and Louisiana, and on July 13 a brief news item appeared stating that "The brick work has commenced on the Capital Hotel extension." In two more weeks, the *Gazette* reported that "Gas pipe is being laid for the purpose of lighting the addition to the Capital Hotel." The hotel management stayed closer to home in furnishing the addition than they had when buying the furniture for the main building.

On October 19, 1877, it was reported that "the furnishings of the new addition to the Capital Hotel," with "about $2,000 worth of furniture," "went toward making it attractive and comfortable." Three weeks later, on November 15, 1877, the Capital Hotel restaurant vacated its room facing on Markham Street and moved into the ground floor of the addition where, the *Gazette* assured its readers "guests can as usual find every delicacy of the season, prepared in the best possible style." At the end of November, "a good pavement has been placed in front of the Capital Hotel Restaurant, fronting Louisiana Street," adding the finishing touch to the addition.

The cost of building the Capital Hotel addition appears to have been financed by the woman who owned the lot it stood on. Elizabeth R. Wright was George C.

Watkins sister-in-law by his second marriage and the daughter to early Arkansas's prominent Sen. William S. Fulton.

The addition was plumbed for wastewater, as the Watkins estate paid for fifty-two feet of twelve-inch sewer pipe, twelve feet of six-inch pipe, and a barrel of cement during this period of construction (Title abstract—Lots 1, 2, 3 Block 78 City of Little Rock Abstract Co.).

Changes to the Main Building

The addition to the rear of the main building was by far the most significant physical change to occur to the building in the year 1877. On the main building that year, the Watkins estate paid for the installation of 675 feet of tin roofing in April in their continual maintenance of the roof (Watkins Probate Catalog). The estate also incurred a major expense preparing one of the shops for a new occupant.

The shop space on the corner of Markham and Louisiana Street had been taken over by Wildberger Confectioners the previous year, who continued to occupy it for the first six months of the year. In July, however, Wildberger was replaced by the Southern Express Company, which needed a vault to conduct their business. Work began on the vault in June, equipped with a tile floor and a gas light fixture.

The year of 1878 bore witness to more maintenance and repairs and several major physical improvements to the building, according to the Watkins Probate Catalog. The roof continued to receive attention, the Watkins estate paying in April and May for thirty gallons of boiled oil and ninety-five pounds of paint for the roof, plus the cost of labor for a man to spend three days cleaning the roof and then $28.40 for painting it. A large section of the roof was tinned in May for $8.04, and thirty-six feet of downspout was replaced in June.

One of the most important changes to the building was begun in May, a change which affected the livability of the structure, bringing it into the modern era and adding greatly to the occupants' convenience and comfort. J. G. Steacy again appears to have been the architect for this work, for he was paid $70.00 the month after it was completed for "Services as Architect on the Capital Hotel Improvements." The improvement: the building received indoor plumbing.

W. H. Woodsmall, who had excavated and laid the sewer for the addition the year previous, again excavated the 230 yards from the hotel to the Arkansas River, hauled the pipe from the railroad and laid it in the ground.

Robert McKay, meanwhile, was building the water closets in the building for his total contract price of $950.00. J. T. Doyle then plumbed the water closets for $425.00, providing a number of connections and installing a total of 204 feet of 1¼-inch pipe and 7½ feet of 1-inch pipe for an additional $68.10. The new facilities must have been fully functional by the twenty-seventh of June, for the Watkins estate paid a $2.00 bill on that day for "pulling down old privy."

The building owners also made a major improvement on the exterior of the building mid-summer by putting in a new sidewalk. The *Gazette* reported on June 5 that "There will soon be a flag sidewalk laid on front of the Capital Hotel, whereat pedestrians will greatly rejoice" (*Arkansas Gazette,* June 5 1978).

A. M. Adams and Son started installing the flagstone sidewalks and curbs, and submitted a final bill on July 15. They had laid "2072 (square) feet flagging in front of Capital Hotel . . . dressing and setting 28 feet curb (and) furnishings and setting 134 feet curb." Their total charge was $488.40 (Watkins Probate Catalog).

The third year of the Capital Hotel's residency in the former Denckla Block is the last year that a significant alteration occurred in the building in the seven-year period that Colonel DeShon ran the hotel. A balcony was added. As can be seen in the early photographs of the Denckla Block and Capital Hotel, the original building did not have any sort of balcony on the façade. The new balcony was compatible visually with the uses of the building, as no shop space needed emphasis over that of its neighbors.

President Grant at the Capital Hotel

In 1880 President Ulysses S. Grant came to Little Rock, in part to reinforce peace and smooth over political cracks and rifts caused by the Brooks-Baxter War. The president received a mixed welcome. Peg Newton Smith, a Little Rock resident, recalls hearing a story about Grant's presidential parade. "When he came through town, the ladies on 9th street were not a bit impressed. The story goes that they brought chairs out onto the lawn and turned them around, so that their backs would be towards the President" (*The Capital Hotel Historic Review Newsletter*, 1983).

Another story retold by a local historian was that Grant, "bone-weary from travel and obliged to stand endless hours in the lobby to greet hordes of well-wishers . . . At last he could stand it no more. Someone suggested that in their innocence, the visitors would be none the wiser if Zeb Ward, the former warden of the state penitentiary and something of a Grant look-alike, stood in for awhile, letting the president retire to his room for a rest. The ruse worked fine until an ex-con, shouting to the entire world that he would know Ward anywhere, gave it all away" (*The Capital Hotel Historic Review*, 1983).

Lifestyle at the New Hotel

> The Capital was beautifully furnished and had daintily figured carpets in every room. Gas provided the lighting system. A magnetized annunciator enabled each guest to request individual room service by merely pushing a button. The Capital provided its guests with a restaurant, bar, barber shop and billiard hall. The 101 elegantly appointed guest chambers carried rates of $2.50 to $4.00 a day.
>
> (*The Capital Hotel Historic Review Newsletter*, 1983)

With the conversion of the building to a hotel, the center shops no longer were merely spaces occupied democratically with their neighbors. Those two central doors were now the formal entrance to the hotel, whose use and identity dominated the building. That reality needed to be translated to the façade, and as previously noted, a small cast-iron balcony added in 1879 above the hotel's office provided the general and ladies' entrance to the hotel. The Fulton saloon was moved to the second floor from its previous corner location on the alley.

The hotel also operated a restaurant for, in offering their rooms on the American plan, meals were included in the price of the room. The first restaurant manager was Frank Mourey, and the restaurant was located just east of the office in shop number 16, "easy of access (to the office) by side doors." The *Gazette* reported of the restaurant that

> . . . all the delicacies of the season (are on the menu) at Mourey's restaurant, 16 Denckla Block, Capital Hotel. Little Rock's popular restaurateur, Frank Mourey, has removed to his new quarters in the Denckla Block, and will hereafter provide edibles for the Capital Hotel guests and the public generally. A more extended notice will be given this deserving establishment in a future issue.
>
> (*Arkansas Gazette,* January 21, 1877)

The *Gazette* never got to publish that more detailed account, however, for it seems that Mr. Mourey ran into some financial difficulties and left town rather abruptly. On the nineteenth of July 1877, the *Gazette* related that "the late employees of Frank Mourey, formerly proprietor of the Capital Hotel restaurant, are anxious as to his whereabouts." He still was not found by August 4, for the paper reported that

> When (glass, china and silver plated ware merchant) Mr. S. Navra's gift drawing occurred last week it was announced that Frank Mourey was the winner of one of the prizes. One of his many creditors has entered a garnishee for the articles won by the absconding Frank . . .
>
> (*Arkansas Gazette,* August 4, 1877)

The Death of Colonel DeShon

In the final months of 1883 and the beginning months of 1884, Col. A. G. DeShon became ill and weakened in strength. In the last two weeks of February 1884, this formerly energetic man slipped in and out of consciousness and lost consciousness entirely before dying on the twenty-eighth day of February of a tumor of the brain. DeShon was fifty-four years old, having been born in upstate New York and working as a railroad conductor until managing the Metropolitan and then Capital Hotel in Little Rock. His obituary described him as having "excellent business ability," and his funeral in the east wing of the Capital Hotel was attended by many prominent Little Rock citizens, who followed to see his casket buried in the venerable Mount Holly cemetery about a dozen blocks away.

DeShon left all his property to his wife, Olive A. DeShon, including his lease to the Capital Hotel (*Arkansas Gazette,* March 4, 1884). On March 11, 1884, she took out an advertisement in the *Gazette* that initiated yet another major period of physical expansion and energetic administration of the Capital Hotel:

Capital Hotel
Furniture and Lease
For Sale

> Circumstances are such that I do not desire to continue the hotel business,
> if I can sell the furniture now in the Capital Hotel at anything like its value.

I have therefore concluded to invite sealed proposals for the purchase of the hotel furniture and the leases thereof and will receive proposals up to and including the 1st day of April, 1884. Parties desiring to examine furniture and leases can do so by application to John McClure, or to myself.

Olive A. DeShon
Little Rock, Arkansas, March 11, 1884

The Second Owners, 1884–1896

Mrs. DeShon opened the bids on the April 1 deadline and picked a buyer the next day. The *Gazette* reported that

> . . . there were several bids, but the largest was made by Mr. J. W. DeShon (not related to the late A. G. DeShon) and Mr. J. F. Calef. Their bid was $28,000 cash, and was accepted. This includes all the furniture in both the west and east wings, and the lease for the hotel, which does not expire yet for 4 years on the new part and 3 years on the old. Cross and Diver were among the other bidders, and their bid was $28,000 on time. Calef and DeShon's bid being for cash, it was accepted. A *Gazette* reporter called on the purchasers yesterday evening, and was informed by them that they would probably take possession today (April 1), and would run the hotel. It is a valuable property, all the best wishes of the *Gazette* for the success are given the gentlemen in their new enterprise. They came to Little Rock from Mobile, Alabama, and have made many friends here and throughout the state during the past 3 years they have been in business as cotton buyers, and will no doubt take hold with the same energy and ability that has so far characterized them.

(*Arkansas Gazette,* April 12, 1884)

Jonathan F. Calef apparently borrowed some of his portion of the twenty-eight-thousand-dollar lease and furniture purchase price from his father, Josiah Bartlett Calef of Mobile, Alabama. In a letter dated August 4, 1884, Calef's father acknowledges receipt of his son's check for $125, "being first quarter's interest on your note for which accept my thanks." The timing of the younger Calef's payment hints that the loan was for his use in the Capital Hotel transaction, as it had been approximately one quarter since Calef purchased the lease. Assuming an interest rate of 10 percent, a $125 quarterly interest payment would indicate a total of $5,000 borrowed.

A prominent merchant in Mobile for over thirty years, the elder Calef acknowledged in his letter receipt of the interest payment, gave news on the unfortunate status of the family's health and then gave his son financial advice:

> I rejoice you have affected [*sic*] such favorable business arrangements. Do try and keep your expenses down and credit up. I want you to succeed this time, as I hear indirectly of persons here prophesying your non-success, saying if old business men and concerns are failing right and left all over the country what can be expected but failure of 2 young men starting off in such an enterprise! I do not know who they are who predict such in success, nor do I wish to know. You must keep your private expenses down and live close

for a while until you are out of debt—Don't feel offended, I do heartily want
you to succeed and prosper, and thereby shut up the mouths of croakers . . .

(*Biographical and Historical Memoirs of Pulaski, Jefferson . . . Counties.*
Chicago: The Goodspeed Pub. Co., 1889)

It would appear that Calef followed his father's advice, for he and his partner
waited until the following year before embarking on major physical improvements
to the hotel. He and DeShon may not have paid for the improvements themselves,
as the Watkins heirs still owned the building. The Watkins probate records, however, do not extend into this period of time, and none of the other information indicates which party financed the improvements.

The *Gazette* reported on September 22, 1885, that

Work was begun yesterday on the Capital Hotel, looking to a remodeling of the whole interior, including the office, billiard-room, bar room and
stairway. "Pete" Mivelaz was engaged in moving out his bar all day to make
room for the carpenters. The plans are for work that will make the hotel modern and handsome in appearance, and furnish a great many conveniences to
the traveling public not now possible. It will be pushed through as rapidly as
practicable.

One of the "many conveniences" that was installed was a new system of lighting.
The *Gazette* reported a month later on October 29: "And still they come. Everybody
wants an electric light. They were put in yesterday at the Capital Hotel . . ." In yet
thirty more days, the newspaper reported that "The Electric Light Co. put a hanging
electric light in front of the Capital Hotel yesterday. And still the electric light boom
continues."

The other improvements were perhaps less revolutionary. A new stairway in the
hotel was started at the beginning of October and completed two weeks later.
Previously a shipment of Vermont marble for hotel improvements had been delivered, and it was used as a floor in the lobby of the hotel. Louis L. Mivelaz, proprietor of the Capital Hotel bar, was reported by the *Gazette* as planning to "add a
number of attractive features to this resort as soon as the hotel improvements are
finished," and Calef and DeShon and a third party petitioned the city council "asking permission to erect a billboard in front of the Capital Hotel," although the newspaper did not report the outcome of the request.

The hotel got a new barber that year, as described in a brief news item in the
July 17 issue of the newspaper: "Barbers Jim and John H. Phillips, will be found on
and after Monday in the Capital Hotel. Look out for the grand opening and fat
man's bath room."

The hotel also ran its own laundry, as is evidenced by another small news item
appearing in August of 1885: "The right person can make satisfactory arrangements
with the proprietors of the Capital Hotel to take charge of the laundry connected
with the hotel." The laundry was probably located in some of the rooms at the back
of the building.

The Capital Hotel restaurant installed its own well during the summer, as
reported by the *Gazette:* "The sound of a well-driver is heard in the rear of the

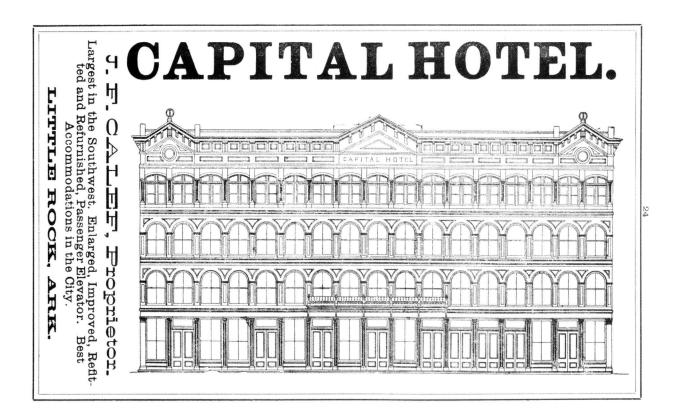

CAPITAL HOTEL.

J. F. CALEF, Proprietor.

Largest in the Southwest, Enlarged, Improved, Refitted and Refurnished, Passenger Elevator. Best Accommodations in the City.

LITTLE ROCK, ARK.

24

Advertisement for the Capital Hotel from the *Little Rock City Directory*, 1890. *(The Butler Center)*

Capital Hotel, where a drive well is being made for the Mivelaz restaurant." Some additional restaurant coverage followed the next month in the newspaper, with the following long article describing its culinary offerings:

The Capital Hotel restaurant has been run for the past four years by Mr. Louis L. Mivelaz, and has become the leading restaurant of the city. There are few restaurant men better posted in their business then Louis Mivelaz. He understands the art of catering to the public in his line to perfection. The great feature about the Mivelaz restaurant is the high standard at which he keeps his table, week in and week out, month in and month out. Mr. Mivelaz will employ none but the best cooks, and pays a personal supervision to every detail. He is to be found at all hours in and about the restaurant attending to the careful attention of his waiters, to the wants of customers. Doing the largest restaurant business in the city, he is able to purchase in large quantities and keeps the best of everything in its season. During the game season now opening there is nothing obtainable that will not be on his bill of fare, and served in excellent style. The delicacies of each season appear on his enticing tables, and it is no wonder that his list of regular boarders as well as transient trade constantly increases. The dining room is handsomely fitted up, is cool and light and a very pleasant place to take a good meal. The table is supplied with the best oysters served in every style, and particular attention is paid to obtaining the best meats in the market. The restaurant is to the rear of the Capital Hotel in the same building. The terms are reasonable, and to all looking for a first-class establishment, this one is recommended as a fine example of that class.

(Arkansas Gazette, September 15, 1885)

In the following year, 1886, the hotel ran an advertisement which included the price of a stay. The difference in price between the American Plan and the European Plan is the difference between having one's meals included with the room and buying them on one's own. Some quick arithmetic shows that the three meals, if that's the total that was included, were figured at $1.50:

The Capital Hotel
Little Rock, Arkansas

J. F. Calef	J. W. DeShon
European Plan	American Plan
50¢ to $1.50	$2.00 to $3.00
per day.	per day.

The favorite Hotel of the State of Arkansas
The Best Accommodations and the Most Reasonable Terms.
The Most Convenient to Business
Its Guests are its References.

In the spring, in April 1887, the *Gazette* reported

Almost a Fire

The Capital Hotel Kitchen Burned This Morning, But It Will Make No Difference to the Accommodation of Guests

An alarm of fire was sounded from the Capital Hotel this morning at 1 o'clock on account of a fire which originated in the kitchen. A *Gazette* reporter arrived on the spot just as the engines arrived and found a scene of wildest excitement. All of the guests of the hotel, about 150 in number, had been awakened and most of them had time to don their garments and grab up their gripsacks and valuables preparatory to decamping. The ladies, some of them with children in their arms, were badly frightened and very excited. But an end to all the excitement came within three minutes after the fire department had gotten to work and within 12 minutes from the time the alarm was sounded by the joyous news that the flames had been extinguished entirely. The kitchen was burned and the windows of the dining room, but the flames did not get into the dining room or any other portion of the hotel, though the walls were heated so that most of the plastering on the walls and ceiling of the room on the side next to the kitchen fell and the room was filled with smoke.

The amount of damages will not go over $500 to $600, and it is understood that this is covered by insurance.

The fire originated from the range in the kitchen, and was discovered by Mr. Will H. Mourning, the night clerk of the hotel, who turned in an alarm immediately, and then with all the bell boys and porters, flew to the upper floors to arouse the sleeping guests. So well did he succeed in this that within 3 minutes every person in the whole building was awake and out of the danger of the fire. Too much cannot be said of the presence of mind and judgement with which he acted on this occasion, as the whole building would soon have been in flames but for the efficient work of the fire department. No less than 50 of the guests were heard lamenting the fact that they would have no breakfast this morning, but the hotel management assured them that they would have breakfast as usual. After this assurance that all the fire was out, the frightened guests all retired again.

Mr. Mivelaz's restaurant, despite the favorable publicity it received in the *Gazette* two years previous, was reported in a letter written to Calef in December 1877, by his former clerk Mr. A. Walker as declining in reputation. Walker, who had gone on to manage the McKibben Hotel in Fort Smith on the Texas border, goes on to discuss at length how a Mr. Irwin will go into competition with the Capital Hotel in Little Rock if Calef is not careful. Irwin, as it would turn out, took over the Capital Hotel from Calef several years later:

My dear Mr. Calef:

I do not know whether you will like what I am going to write you but I conscientiously think it my duty. There is one of the largest and loudest kicks against the Capital Hotel that you ever heard[.] I never realized it until I got out of the office but now everyone has damned the place that I have as yet met even people who I thought were our best friends[.] the kick is not against the hotel but against the dining room[,] the prices and the food they get[.] I do not tell you this to worry you because I know you have enough to worry about but I tell it to caution you to look out that there will be a fine American plan hotel in Little Rock in less than 12 months—Now you are liked respected and have a big following[.] why should you not take time by the forelock and have the house[?] You have good backing and I think you must admit that a first class American hotel will pay, I feel confident of it. You can get a good steward at 150$ per month from New York, who can relieve you entirely of all cares of the kitchen and you purchase if you felt so inclined although I find my steward a better purchaser than I am. Little Rock is the only town in the state and I know pretty well what she can do and what a first class house can do. But of course it would cost money, but it could be easily raised right in the town. William Kerrgin[?] late superintendent of MoPac expressed himself to me and said he would take 50,000$ worth[.] let Roots and others raise the money and you lease it. Meeker owns what I consider to be the location of all locations Cor. 2nd. and Broadway Streets. Custom House on one corner Court House opposite which would insure a good neighborhood[.] Broadway is the finest street in Little Rock for a hotel as it is the widest making a beautiful approach to an elegant building, their Markham will in a year or so be taken up by wholesale grocers as a city always moves from the river. Get this location with proper building and you are ok. I enclose you a letter from Irwin of the Huntington[.] he has money and backing so look out for him as he is carried away with L Rock as a point and is determined to get in there[.] he would not touch the Dressing[?] but will get capatalists [*sic*] to build, of course this is strictly private especially this letter[.] I have answered it and told him that for four or five months that you actually did nothing and that it was only for a month or two that the Capital did any trade. I told him this because I did not wish to in any way injure you who have been so kind to me and by the by I must thank you for the assistance you rendered my wife. Trade is exceedingly dull up here[.] I am doing the entire bulk of the trade but that is not enough to keep my poor little 38 rooms full[.] hotels are over done in this town. The Main ought to do the business but it don't[.] it has been fitted up very handsomely but the proprietors are not making their salt. Best regards to Mrs. Calef and yourself.

Yours, A Walker

*(Biographical and Historical Memoirs
of Pulaski, Jefferson . . . Counties)*

The 1887 the city directory shows the same constellation of building occupants as in the year before, with all but two of these occupants appearing to occupy their previous locations. The billiard hall, next door to the east of the office appears to have been supplanted by a real estate agent. It is also interesting to note that two businesses, the saloon and a ticket broker, listed themselves for the first time in 1887 as being located in the "Rotunda, Capital Hotel." This area is presumably the one-story-high space at the rear of the center area of the building labeled as having a glass roof on the fire insurance map.

Calef bought out his partner J. W. DeShon the following year in 1888, becoming the sole owner of a business described as

> . . . a well-built brick structure, fitted up in an excellent manner with all the modern improvements, such as elevator, annunciator, electric light, etc. The hotel contains 104 large, light, airy and well-ventilated rooms, the bed chambers being fitted up and furnished in the best possible style as is also the entire establishment. The large, handsome and commodious dining-room has a seating capacity for some 300 guests, the tables of which are everything that even an epicure could desire, being ladened with everything in the way of substantials and delicacies the season's market affords and served up in a very tempting manner, the culinary department being looked after by an A-1 chef, the best that could be obtained. A well-regulated Bar and Billiard Hall is carried on in connection with the house for the benefit of the guests, and everything is done to make life pleasant and happy while sojourning under the hospitable roof of the Capital . . . its guests at all times leave with regret and return with pleasure.

(Rambles in Manufacturing and Commercial Circles in Little Rock.
Memphis: Historical and Descriptive Publishing, 1888.)

On October 9, the *Gazette* reported a request made by the Capital Hotel at a city council meeting, reflecting another addition to the rear of the hotel. A petition was read by council members W. F. Wright, J. F. Calef, and Dr. C. Watkins, asking to continue the building of an elevator shaft in the rear of the Capital Hotel, the same to be covered with corrugated iron. The petition also stated that the contractor, William McDowell, had men fined in the police court for a violation of the

This map of Little Rock in 1887 shows the layout of the city and its proximity to the Arkansas River. Among the buildings which are listed are the Capital Hotel (L) as well as the "Colored Church" (Y) and the "U.S. Arsenal" (I). *(Courtesy Arkansas History Commission)*

A. Arkansas State Capitol.
B. Pulaski County Court House.
C. City Hall.
D. Post Office.
E. Arkansas School for Blind.
F. Arkansas Deaf Mute Institute
G. State Penitentiary.
H. Mount Holly Cemetery.
I. U S Arsenal.
J. West End Park.

K. Gazette Building
L. Capital Hotel.
M. Convent.
N. Catholic Cathedral.
O. Episcopal Church.
P. 1st Presbyterian Church.
Q. 2nd Presbyterian Church.
R. Board of Trade.
S. Christian Church.
T. Cumberland Presbyterian Church

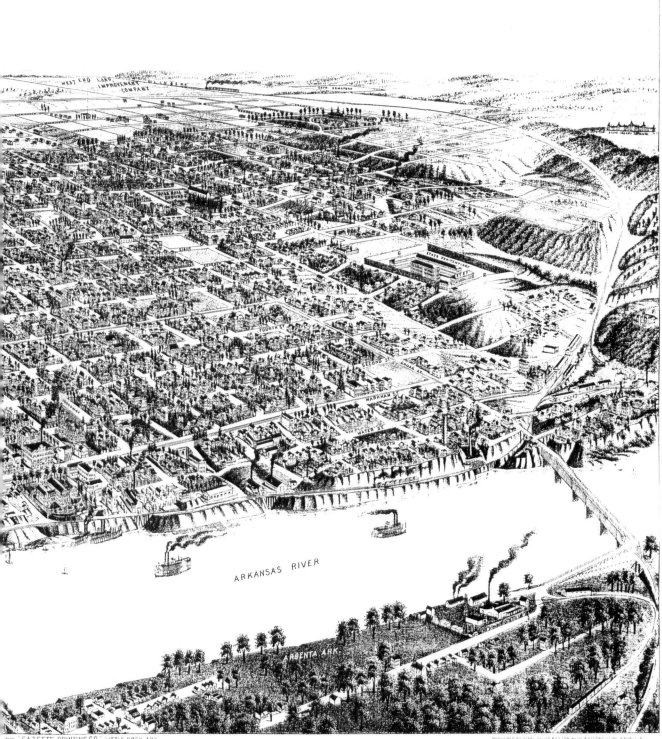

Another photograph of the
Capital Hotel after the addition
of the fourth floor in 1890.
*(Courtesy Arkansas History
Commission)*

ordinance requiring to first have a permit. The permit, on motion of city council
member, Mr. Wolf, was granted.

The Addition of the Fourth Floor, 1890

Calef was responsible for the second major expansion of the Capital Hotel
building since its construction in 1874. Over the winter of 1889 and the spring of
1890, a fourth floor was added to the original three-story building.

Observing the hotel at present it is obvious the design of the additional floor
blends with the lower portion of the building. The front façade repeats the classical design of the first three floors, but instead of cast iron, it is constructed of sheet
metal. The sides are made of brick, and the fourth-floor windows on the Louisiana
Street side mirror the rounded arches of the windows below with arches more flat-
tened in shape. The top of the building is capped with an elaborate bracketed cornice with pedimented gables at the corners, and the central flagpole and classical
monogram are retained and placed above the central entrance on top of the new
fourth-floor cornice.

The iron balcony added in 1879 was also expanded. It is still located at the center of the building above the hotel's main entrance, but was lengthened to become five windows long. It is supported on the front by six iron columns, more slender in diameter than their counterparts on the building's façade. The new balcony extended over the entire sidewalk to the street and large canvas awnings at either end hung down to display lettering reading "Capital Hotel."

Several other improvements were noted in the *Gazette* in the early months of 1890. The newspaper reported that "Joseph C. Herold, the railroad ticket broker, has greatly improved the appearance of his counter at the Capital Hotel by inserting in its sides several handsomely painted glass panels" (*Arkansas Gazette,* January 28, 1890).

The addition of electric fans in the hotel in May 1890 was also noted, along with a whimsical application of their turbulence: "Revolving fans that reduce the temperature to a point that makes life worth living were put into operation in the Capital Hotel restaurant and bar." Seven days, later, "I will now give you an imitation of an ocean breeze, remarked one of Louis Ogier's revolving fans as it lifted Joe Herold's derby from his brow and sent it rolling across the marble floor of the Capital Hotel lobby" (*Arkansas Gazette,* May 29, 1890).

Work was also being done on the interior. At the end of May, the *Gazette* reported that "Graining is an art and the painters engaged in embellishing the interior of the Capital Hotel, appear to be masters at it" (*Arkansas Gazette,* July 15, 1890). Graining is a process where stains and pigments are applied to a wood surface using fine and various sized metal combs to make a less expensive wood appear to be a richly grained

This drawing of the New Capital Hotel shows the addition of the fourth floor which was added in 1890. It is interesting to note the mix of early cars, a tram, and horse-drawn vehicles, typical of Little Rock at the turn of the century. *(Courtesy Arkansas History Commission)*

and expensive material. It is a difficult, demanding, and now-rare art, with individual craftsmen leaving their personal signatures in their styles and techniques.

The latest physical improvement mentioned by the newspaper for the Capital Hotel in 1890 was a brief snippet of news stating that "The Capital Hotel is to have fire escapes," identifying neither their type of construction nor location on the building (*Arkansas Gazette,* July 15, 1890).

With the addition of the fourth floor, the last major physical changes to the Capital Hotel until after the turn of the century had been effected. The uses of the shop-spaces remained basically the same as in the past, with some minor shifting and modification.

CHAPTER TWO

THE CAPITAL HOTEL,
1908 TO 1977

Little Rock between 1900 and 1916 was, like much of the country, in a period of growth. "Population expansion, property annexation, and physical development combined to thrust the city into a modern urban center" (Jim Lester and Judy Lester. *Greater Little Rock*). During this period the Capital Hotel was bought from the heirs of Judge Watkins by Henry Franklin Auten.

Auten, like Denckla, was a Yankee. Auten had lived in St. Johns, Michigan, where he was a successful attorney. Attracted by what he saw to be a significant real estate investment opportunity in Little Rock, H. F. Auten sold his law practice, moved to Little Rock and eventually developed the bulk of property today known as Pulaski Heights.

Tom Dillard in an article ("A Man Who Could Not Stand Still. "*Pulaski County Historical Review* 29 Spring 1981) about Auten said, "Auten's move to Arkansas, like so much of his life, is shrouded in mystery. His widow wrote in 1939 that Auten 'sometime about 1883, while on a train, picked up a little folder . . . and was deeply impressed by a paragraph related to Arkansas.'" It must have been extraordinary sales copy, because shortly thereafter, Auten came to Little Rock.

So why another Yankee? Dillard comments: "Without a class of native businessmen willing to pursue speculative economic development, the responsibility fell to a large degree upon the shoulders of newly arrived Northern immigrants."

Actually, it probably was not so much a lack of entrepreneurial spirit as it was the inability of the South to fund its own expansion. The South after the Civil War was cash-poor, and it took money from outside the state to build railroads and commercial developments like the Capital Hotel and Pulaski Heights.

In any event, Auten moved to Little Rock in 1890, opened a law practice, and for a while became highly involved in politics to the point where he actually ran for governor on the Republican Party ticket. Dillard describes "this Yankee entrepreneur" urging the state populace to embrace industrialism and free enterprise: "he decried the lack of industry in the state, asking why Arkansas cotton and timber were sent out of state for processing."

Auten's message was not accepted, and he suffered overwhelming defeat in the 1898 election. From that point on, Auten turned his attention in earnest to business. He would show in deed what he had preached from the political pulpit. One of his first significant business ventures was to help build streetcar service to Pulaski Heights. This was a key event: "Prior to the advent of the streetcar, the expansion of cities was limited by their residents' need to live within walking distance of shopping areas and places of employment as relatively few people could afford the luxury of maintaining private transportation (horses or carriages). Inexpensive public transportation,

Henry Franklin Auten.
(The Butler Center)

in the form of the streetcar, provided the means by which large numbers of city dwellers were able to live farther from the city, thus allowing for the development of suburbs" (Cheryl G. Nichols. "The Development of Pulaski Heights." *Pulaski County Historical Review* 30 Spring 1982).

Auten's real estate development in Pulaski Heights was an immediate success, and he turned his roving entrepreneurial eye to other related projects including the Capital Hotel.

Auten and the Purchase of the Capital Hotel

The sale of the Capital Hotel to Auten was reported in the *Arkansas Gazette* on July 25, 1908, and gives us a glimpse of the role the Capital had played as a stage for political events.

Passing of a Famous Hotel

*With the Closing of the Capital in This City,
Historic Hostelry Will Pass Out of Existence.*

Scene of Political Battles

*For Nearly Half a Century, The Capital
Was the Political Headquarters of the State.*

BY THE ARKANSAW TRAVELER.

The passing of one of the most famous and historic hostelries in the State of Arkansas is heralded by the announcement that the old Capital hotel of Little Rock will close its doors tonight. There are many older buildings in Little Rock, but there are none which have been more closely connected with the public life of the state during the past 40 years.

For nearly half a century, previous to the opening of the new Hotel Marion, the Capital was the leading hotel of Little Rock. During all that time it was the political headquarters of the state and within its walls has been settled the destinies of almost every politician that has sought office in Arkansas during the past 40 years. If walls had mouths as well as ears, those of the old Capital hotel could tell tales which would be more interesting than any history ever written. From rooms in the Capital have been pulled wires which have elected governors, presidents of the Senate and speakers of the House of Representatives, to say nothing of numerous other officers of major or minor importance. More of the state's history has probably been made in the seclusion of the Capital Hotel rooms than in the legislative halls of the state house.

Scene of Big Political Battle

One of the most famous political battles which were waged within the walls of the hotel was that between J. D. Walker of Fayetteville and R. W. Johnson, father of Col. Ben S. Johnson of this city, who were candidates for the United States Senate in 1879, to succeed the Republican incumbent, Stephen W. Dorsey. Walker had headquarters in one end of the hotel and Johnson in the other and from their representative rooms the campaign was directed. This campaign, which resulted in victory for Walker, was one of the most memorable political campaigns in the history of the state. This was only one of innumerable political battles that were waged in the old hotel.

The Capital has also been the temporary home of many distinguished citizens of the United States. President Grant was entertained at the Capital on the occasion of his visit to Little Rock, and practically every prominent man who has visited the city in the past 40 years has been a guest at the hotel.

Many of the stirring scenes of the Brooks-Baxter war were enacted in front of the building. It formed the dividing lines between the contending forces. The middle ground, immediately in front of the present hotel entrance was occupied by the federal troops who were attempting to prevent a clash between the Brooks and Baxter forces. The officers of the federal troops established headquarters in the Capital Hotel building and the soldiers occupied the street and the alleyway at the side of the old city hall, directly across the street from the hotel entrance.

Early Proprietors of Hotel

One of the earliest proprietors of the hotel was A. G. DeShon, an old conductor on the Little Rock and Memphis Railroad. Later the hotel passed under the management of Calef and DeShon, the latter being no relative of the first proprietor, A.G. DeShon. Later John F. Calef bought out his partner and conducted the hotel. Louis Mivelaz held a lease on the property for some time and other changes were made in the management until 1895, when Joseph W. Irwin became the manager. He remained in charge until August 1, 1907, when the property was sold to Chris Ledwidge of this city. The consideration was stated to be $150,000. A few weeks ago it was announced that the property had again been sold, the new purchasers being represented by H. F. Auten of this city.

Mr. Auten will obtain possession of the property on August 1 and he had determined to close the hotel at that time. Mr. Auten states that the new owners have not determined what they will do with the property. It may be remodeled and reopened as a hotel or it may be converted into stores and offices. This will probably be determined within the next two or three weeks.

Auten was initially somewhat undecided whether to continue to run the Capital as a hotel or to convert it back into office or retail space as it had been when Denckla first owned it. Evidently Auten thought the growth in Little Rock could sustain two hotels, for in less than a month, the *Gazette* heralded the following news:

Capital Hotel to Be Rebuilt

At a Cost of $250,000 the "New Capital" Will Be Made One of the Finest in the South

To Begin Work in a Week

Finishing to Be Elaborate, and Lobby to Be the Largest in the Entire South

The Capital hotel is to be rebuilt at once, the estimated cost being $250,000, and the new modern fireproof structure, six stories high, will have the dignified name of "New Capital." This announcement was made yesterday by H. F. Auten and Chris Ledwidge who are in the company that will finance the proposition. There has been much guesswork and many surmises as to the fate of the historic building and the *Gazette* gives the first authorized correct statement.

It is proposed by the promoters to make the new hotel the finest in the state of Arkansas. A two-story, colonial-style porch will be built on the Markham Street side, and both the Markham and Louisiana street fronts will be of plate glass. The lobby will be 100 feet deep and 50 feet wide. It is claimed this will be the largest lobby of any hotel in the South.

The interior finishings in the lobby will be marble up to the fresco of the ceiling. The staircase will be of solid white marble and will front the main cafe.

The cafe will have 2,000 feet of floor space and will be separated from the lobby only by a plate glass partition. It is claimed this will be not only beautiful, but will result in the cafe's having a natural light. The grill room will front on Louisiana Street. The cafe grill room and barbershop, like the lobby will be of marble wainscoting to the fresco work of the ceiling and will have tile flooring.

There will be a ladies' entrance on Markham Street.

In the old building, there is a dining hall on the second floor. This dining hall will be converted into a banquet and convention hall and will be finished in marble and art glass.

Extensive parlors on the second floor will open directly on the porch, and will face the two-story high lobby. Above the parlors will be a dome, finished elaborately in art glass and electrical appliances. The hotel will have 200 sleeping rooms and more than half will be equipped with bath.

Building Will Be Reinforced

The building itself will be reinforced with iron and concrete and made strong enough to add two more stories. All of the ancient wooden work will be removed, and the building will be made as near fireproof as concrete and iron can make it.

George R. Mann is the architect and W. R. Stewart is the contractor. The contractor will begin work within a week and finish the building as soon as possible.

The old furniture in the hotel will be sold at once, and the "New Capital" will be furnished new throughout.

Its Central Location

It was pointed out by the promoters that the site of the Capital is practically the center of the city. Ten banking institutions are within a block of the building. The post office, city hall, courthouse, Hotel Marion and Southern Trust Building are all near the site of the Capital, and it is pointed out that the remodeled building will be the permanent center of the city.

The "Men Behind"

"The men behind this project are amply able to carry it out," said one of the promoters yesterday, "and Little Rock, with two such hotels as the New Capital and the Marion, will be made famous as the best hotel city in the entire South." Among the men financially interested in the project are: F. B. Hollenberg, Bishop John B. Morris, W. E. Lenon, W. M. Kavanaugh, Oscar Davis. T. M. Mehaffy, T. H. Bunch, J. R. Vinson, W. R. Stewart, George R. Mann, W. W. Dickinson, Chris Ledwidge, Lewis Rhoton, H. K. Cochran, W. S. Mitchell, C. S. Stifft, H. F. Auten, Julian Blass, Ike Kempner and other whose names have been withheld. The promoters have even secured a manager for the new hotel, but they declined yesterday to give his name. It was stated, however, that he is a man of wide experience in the hotel business.

(*Arkansas Gazette,* August 15, 1908)

George R. Mann's Renovation

George R. Mann, the architect responsible for the remodeling design, is a significant figure in Arkansas's architectural heritage. Mann came to Arkansas in 1900 from Missouri, bringing with him a design for a new capitol. He was well received by the governor and legislature, and they selected him without the bother of hosting a design competition as was the practice in most other states, to design the Capitol. Mann's list of other Arkansas buildings is impressive and includes the *Arkansas Gazette* and Donaghey Buildings, the Pulaski County Courthouse addition, and the Marion Hotel. His alteration of the Capital Hotel storefronts, lobbies, and rotunda provided the hotel with a modernizing facelift and opened up the lobby space into a more unified and impressive area. The idea of adding two additional floors was, however, abandoned.

In the same year that the Capital reopened, the Marion Hotel—also a Mann design—also opened for business. The Marion, with 175 rooms, lavish parlors, ornamented lobby, and ballroom, was considered to be the most elegant hotel in the city. In spite of the competition across the street, the Capital continued to prosper and flourish up until the Great Depression in 1929.

The Death of H. F. Auten

Tom Dillard writes, "The bright surface of Auten's life gave no hint of the tragedy that was to come. In the spring of 1918, he was forced to bed with an illness that resulted in gradual paralysis . . . In May he was taken to Hot Springs where he went into a coma" ("A Man Who Could Not Stand Still").

Auten died on May 23, 1918.

From its renovation and reopening in 1908 until Auten's death on May 23, 1918, the Capital Hotel had continued to prosper. Auten's fortune did not service his debt, or much of his business ventures had been financed on credit. "As the estate was gradually liquidated it became clear that the Auten heirs would be left with only modest inheritances." In fact by 1932 the entire estate had a balance of $9.98 ("A Man Who Could Not Stand Still").

"Mrs. Patricia Aderhold, granddaughter of H. F. Auten, believes that the family was able to save the Capital Hotel only through the efforts of her father, Lawrence" ("A Man Who Could Not Stand Still").

The Capital Hotel: Life of the Party and the "Party"

Pauline Hoetzel, a Little Rock resident, recalls the Capital Hotel during the first world war: "During vacations, I attended many parties given by companies and groups stationed at Camp Pike near here. The Louisiana State University men and others had many Saturday night dances there in the ballroom and the mezzanine. It was decorated with palms in large urns all around the room and paper duplicates of the tiger, the university mascot, hung on the walls. Between dances and at intermission, couples sat in overstuffed leather chairs on the mezzanine or strolled onto the balcony which overlooked the entrance. The Bordeaux Drug Store in the downstairs corner of Markham and Louisiana was full of couples. The music at these dances was usually jazz" (*The Capital Hotel Register Newsletter*, 1982).

"Years later, Pauline headed up the Women's Division for the gubernatorial campaign of Sid McMath. The campaign was run from the Capital Hotel and

Pauline recalls that the rooms were alive with political activity. 'Many strange people came and went and there was always a great deal of secretive guesswork as to who they were and as to whether they were converts to our cause or spies for the opposition'" (*The Capital Hotel Register Newsletter*, 1982).

Gibson Discount Stores and the Capital Hotel

Jim and Judy Lester write, "Hoover's American dream had turned into a nightmarish fantasy haunted by the pleading eyes of apple vendors and vacant stares of desperate people waiting in breadlines. With the arrival of the 1930s, Little Rock and the rest of America began the ordeal of the great Depression. In Arkansas's capital city a drought generated by seventy-one rainless days during the summer of 1930 accentuated the later business failures, mortgage foreclosures and bank closings. Employers reduced salaries, fired employees, and hung the 'going out of business' signs in their windows" (Jim Lester and Judy Lester. *Greater Little Rock*).

It was a grim time that tested the endurance and tenacity of the nation.

One unique business personality who personally fought the economic downturn and managed to establish a business was H. R. Gibson. In the height of the depression amidst the sea of bankruptcy and insolvency, Gibson had the audacity to establish a small shop on the ground floor of the Capital Hotel.

"I drove up this street and down that one. Man, I'd never seen so many vacant buildings in m' life. I'd venture to say seventy-five per cent of the b'iness buildings was vacant. Little Rock had been hit bad" (Robert W. Lawrence. *This Man Gibson*. Dallas: Gospel Teachers Publications, Inc., 1974). From his office in the Capital he employed a dedicated team of traveling salesmen.

"Knowing the country folk as he did, Gibson gathered his sales force together and told them that the surrounding small towns never had banks. The people in these communities kept their money under the floor in mason jars. They would need goods and would have ready cash to pay for them. His strategy worked. He sold his merchandise statewide . . . Mr. Gibson moved four times within the Capital Hotel. Each time he moved into a larger space while he increased his merchandise lines. Today, Gibson's Discount Stores reach across the country. A success story rooted at the capital Hotel" (*The Capital Hotel Register Newsletter*, 1982).

The Sale of the Capital Hotel to Amelia Cassinelli

Amelia and Elizabeth Cassinelli were sisters, part of a large, northern Italian family with various retail interests in Little Rock and North Little Rock. One of Amelia and Elizabeth's establishments was the Brass Rail restaurant which was across the street from the Capital. One of the regular patrons of the Brass Rail was Lawrence Auten. The Cassinelli sisters and Auten began talking and eventually negotiated a deal; the Cassinellis bought the Capital in 1947. For the next three decades (1947 to 1977), the Capital was owned and operated by the sisters.

Initially, the Capital remained the crown jewel in Little Rock's society, entertainment and hospitality establishment. Parker Westbrook, then special assistant to

Front cover of *This Man Gibson*. H. R. Gibson was a colorful, high-spirited, successful businessman and entrepreneur who founded Gibson Department Stores after the Depression. In the height of economic downturn, Gibson started his first store on the ground floor of the Capital Hotel. *(Reproduced with permission from York College, York, Nebraska)*

Sen. William Fulbright, remembers the Capital as being a hub of social and political activity. "Senator Fulbright was a personal friend of the Cassinelli sisters. He ran his first campaign out of an office located in the Capital. He also had his office at the Capital in his later bid for re-election."

Five years after the Capital had been restored, Howard Coan, a reporter for the *Arkansas Democrat* interviewed the younger sister, Elizabeth, after Amelia had died in 1976. The article, published on November 8, 1988, gives some interesting and essential background on the Cassinelli proprietorship of the hotel:

> From her home (in North Little Rock), where she was born 81 years ago, Elizabeth Cassinelli explained how two sisters without any hotel management experience became involved in such a business, and how they survived some difficult times.
>
> Her father, Louis, came to St. Louis with his father and one sister at the age of seven from a small town near Genoa, Italy.
>
> Louis left his St. Louis home as a teen-ager and, after traveling and working in several parts of the country, ended up in Little Rock in 1879 at the age of 39.
>
> "I have no idea why he came to Little Rock," Cassinelli said. Her father bought some inexpensive land in North Little Rock to grow fruits and vegetables, which he then sold in his store at 205 Main Street in Little Rock.
>
> Later, he bought more land in the North Little Rock area and became a prominent real estate developer. At the age of 48, he married Italian-born Elizabeth Bertola, an 18-year old who lived with her family in a town near Morrilton.
>
> "Papa corresponded with Mama by letter in Italian. He didn't even meet her in person until he proposed," Cassinelli noted.

Large Family

> The couple had six boys and two girls in the next 17 years, with Elizabeth being the last child, 10 years younger than her sister, Amelia.
>
> At 16, Amelia was forced to quit high school to help her ailing father in his real estate business. He died several years later, and Amelia was on her own.
>
> In the next several decades, Amelia became one of the area's first successful female real estate developers.
>
> "She was the business-woman. I wasn't." her sister said.
>
> For a time, Elizabeth studied in Cincinnati and Memphis, Tennessee to be an opera singer. But with the start of the Great Depression, she returned home to help in the real estate business.

1940 Quest Began

> The path toward buying the Capital Hotel began in 1940 when the Cassinellis acquired the Brass Rail restaurant across Markham Street from the hotel.
>
> Pulaski County Circuit Judge Lawrence Auten, who had inherited the Capital Hotel from his father, dined frequently at the restaurant. "That's how we got to know Judge Auten."
>
> According to Cassinelli, Auten had not been spending much time with his hotel, which was declining both in popularity and reputation.
>
> Auten decided to sell the Capital to the Cassinelli sisters.
>
> Amelia's name was on the ownership papers, but "what was hers, was mine. We lived for each other," Cassinelli said.
>
> Amelia invested money in the hotel, including the installation of new flooring, plumbing and bath tiles.
>
> "We tried to build it back, and we did," Cassinelli said.

Hard Worker

"Amelia worked like a dog. She invested money—no telling how much she put into it. She was always doing something."

But whatever money she took out, Amelia reinvested in the hotel. They never made much money on the business, Cassinelli said.

In those days, the hotel charged $4 a night for a room without bath, and $6 a night with bath.

In 1962, the Little Rock Housing Authority paid more than $225,000 for what was known as the Cassinelli Building, which included the Brass Rail and a liquor store in the 100 block of Markham. The Cassinelli family also owned three other nearby buildings, which they rented out to businesses.

These parcels along with some other property, ultimately became the sites for the State Convention center and the Excelsior Hotel.

After the sale, Elizabeth worked full time at the hotel which now also included the relocated liquor store.

Bedded by Illness.

In the early 1970s, Amelia was forced to remain at home because of a kidney ailment and Elizabeth took charge.

At that time, Amelia also began discussions with Little Rock architect Edwin Cromwell about buying the hotel, Cassinelli said. "My sister wanted so much money. They couldn't get together on the price."

The Rest of the Story

What is striking about the *Democrat* article is that there was no detailed mention of the other Cassinelli family members: there were, after all, six brothers in addition to the two Cassinelli sisters. Andrea Cassinelli, former owner of the award-winning four-star restaurant on Main Street in North Little Rock was Amelia and Elizabeth's niece and actually lived in the same ancestral household in North Little Rock. Many other Cassinelli family members were involved with running the family business that gave Amelia the wherewithal to eventually buy the Capital Hotel.

"My father was one of eight children," said Andrea in an interview. "Andrew Cassinelli . . . he was number seven, and the sixth of six boys. Shortly after I was born, in 1940, he and his brother, Richard, which was the brother next to him in age, went into business together and started a vending company. And that vending company is still in business today. They also did a few other things together. They had some bars, which was pretty typical of the time of the Italians, nothing out of the ordinary there."

Jim Lester and Judy Lester in their book *Greater Little Rock* write, "During the twentieth century . . . the Capital Hotel steadily declined into a cheap flophouse and underground brothel until the early 1980s when a group of new investors launched an elaborate plan to renovate the hotel and return the structure to its former glory."

Andrea, responding to allegations that Amelia ran a brothel said: "I believe she chose to overlook that. I'm not saying that sort of activity didn't go on . . . it does in any hotel. But Amelia always said her job was to rent rooms . . ."

So rent rooms Amelia did, if only at times by the hour. Perhaps desperate

Above: This photograph of Elizabeth Cassinelli was taken by an *Arkansas Democrat* newspaper reporter in 1988. Elizabeth and her sister, Amelia, ran the Capital Hotel from 1947 to 1977. (Arkansas Democrat-Gazette)

Left: Elizabeth *(left)* and Amelia *(right)* Cassinelli on the grounds of the Cassinelli estate. The Cassinelli sisters were part of a family that immigrated from northern Italy to Arkansas and ran a variety of retail businesses including a fruit stand in North Little Rock. *(Photograph courtesy of Andrea Cassinelli)*

financial necessity and the very location of the property in a deteriorating part of town resulted in the less than desirable clientele. Elizabeth put it this way in the '88 interview: "We weren't a first class hotel. It was for out-of-town tourists and other people."

But it wasn't just the Capital Hotel that was declining. On May 10, 1970, the *Arkansas Gazette* ran an article that quoted several state legislators who bemoaned quality of hotel accommodations.

> The defunct Hotel Marion may once have been what most political observers always considered it to be—the place where major legislative decisions were made. But several years before its closing, April 30, it ceased to be "the place" for Arkansas legislators to transact business after the House and Senate closed . . . Representative Joseph T. Hamilton of Harrison said he hadn't stayed at the Marion for years, preferring the Sam Peck . . . Representative Bobby G. Newman of Smackover agreed—"It was not a central meeting place anymore." Mrs. Dorothy M. Allen of Brinkley, a state senator and long term Marion customer will move to the Grady Manning . . . Senator Ralph Hudson of Harrison is shopping around. "My wife and I are not real sure where we may be. We might stay at the Coachman's Inn . . . I think Little Rock has slipped in not having another place ready" . . .

Adjacent to this article the *Gazette* printed another piece with the headline: "Owner of Capital Attributes Survival to the Management":

> Diagonally across West Markham and Louisiana Streets from the Marion Hotel stands the old Capital Hotel, one of the city's architectural and historic landmarks, which, from all external appearances, should have fallen victim to economics long before its much larger neighbor.
>
> The difference, said Miss Amelia Cassinelli, owner of the Capital, must be one of personal versus corporate management.
>
> "When the owner operates a place themselves," she said, "they are more conservative. It's like running a household. The wife can do it more economically than a maid."
>
> And then there's the minimum wage law to contend with, she said. "To get four hours of work out of employees nowadays you have to work 'em eight." With her Capital Hotel being smaller (about 90 rooms compared with 350 for the Marion), "you can be more observant," she said.
>
> Miss Cassinelli said she was gradually modernizing the Capital, installing tiled baths in bathless rooms and readying the ground floor coffee shop for reopening . . . The ground-floor shops are vacant, but Miss Cassinelli is seeking appropriate tenants. She has had the usual inquiries from prospective candidates about leasing space, but the change in the ticket-closing date to later in the year has delayed those commitments.
>
> The Capital has only two or three permanent guests, and Miss Cassinelli said the Hotel doesn't cater to them. "We're small, and we want as much income as we can get—no weekly or monthly rates."

The Cassinelli family were hard-working people, with extremely high standards. It was in some ways a tragedy that the sisters simply could not afford to operate the Capital in a manner which they wanted. The Capital was in desperate need of repair

Andrew and Elizabeth
Cassinelli with Ed Cromwell at
the one-hundredth anniversary
of the Capital Hotel in 1972.
*(Cromwell Architects and
Engineers, Inc.)*

and in the end Amelia, despite her hard-nosed business acumen, was unable to fund significant restoration work.

Larry Martin, a Cromwell employee and consultant at the time, remembers meeting both Amelia and Elizabeth: "Ms. Elizabeth had always been the baby, always acted like the baby. She loved to flirt in public. They had a nice home in North Little Rock. Ms. Amelia I think was in her late eighties and Ms. Elizabeth was in her early eighties when I first met them. Rather late in life for flirtations, but it was a mindset. You never saw anybody check in or out of the place except for an hour or two at a time. I don't know how they kept it open. They rented the pool hall. They were having a real tough time, but they were fiercely proud of the place. They were proud of it; it was a part of their family. They remembered the glory days and they knew that it would come back. They really wanted to be part of it."

It seems that Elizabeth was a master storyteller and a flirt, adept at creating wonderful fantasies. Not all is known about the truth surrounding Elizabeth, her sister, and what the Capital might or might not have been. But whatever the circumstances surrounding the internal family struggles, the Cassinelli family helped to preserve the Capital Hotel, which might have otherwise been torn down.

Amelia died in 1974 and this allowed Elizabeth to come to terms on the sale of the property to Ed Cromwell. In 1983, when the restoration was complete, Elizabeth was led into the lobby, now completely restored to its early grandeur. Upon witnessing the hotel in its near mint condition again, the now eighty-something Cassinelli burst into tears. "They had cameras on me and I started to cry. I said Amelia wanted the hotel to look like this. She wanted a real first class hotel."

A party was held to commemorate the one-hundredth year of the Capital Hotel. By this time the hotel was in extreme disrepair, and party guests wore coats because the heating and plumbing had been turned off. (Arkansas Democrat-Gazette)

Edwin B. Cromwell

Ed Cromwell is the pivotal figure in the saving and restoration of the Capital Hotel. Tom Honeycut—a reporter for *Arkansas Business* in 1985—said, "He carries himself as the old Southern gentleman, with a shock of white hair that brings to mind the late poet and Lincoln biographer, Carl Sandburg" (*Arkansas Business,* April 29, 1985).

In my visits and interviews with Cromwell, the retired architect was clear about what he wanted: "This book you're writing . . . I don't really care if I'm in it, but I

Edwin B. Cromwell. *(Arkansas Business, Andrew Kilgore)*

want you to be sure to include everyone who helped and wanted the Capital Hotel restored. There are so many people . . . people in the business community, people in government like Senator Pryor. Writers and reporters like Harryette Hodges . . . and just private ordinary citizens whom I didn't know at all but who took the time to write to me and supported the project in their own way. This is *their* story, not mine. Don't write too much about me or I'll have to leave town."

In fact much has already been written about Ed Cromwell and his campaign to save the Capital. On December 19, 1983, the *Arkansas Gazette* ran a story:

> After years of disappointments and setbacks, he (Cromwell) and a cast
> of hundreds will deliver to the city a hotel with aesthetic and architectural
> interest; with a history that parallels some of Arkansas' most important
> events, and with a charm that reflects the affection that has been bestowed
> on it. "It's not really a private building in the real sense . . . the people of
> Little Rock not only wanted this restoration. They demanded it." Cromwell
> says his importance in saving the Capital is overblown—that others had just
> as much to do with it as he did. But over period of decades he is the thread
> that connects numerous persons and events to the renovation.
>
> (*Arkansas Gazette,* December 19, 1983)

This modest, understated demeanor is quintessential Cromwell. A Princeton graduate, Cromwell was a man who worked hard throughout his life, prospered in good times, and survived some really tough years. His most significant contribution is perhaps the impact he had on the landscape of downtown Little Rock, an impact that goes far beyond the immediate project of just saving the Capital Hotel.

When I interviewed those who worked for and around Cromwell over the years, the word "visionary" seemed to be used consistently. Bill Worthen, director of the Arkansas History Museum (formerly the Territorial Restoration Commission), which Cromwell headed for fifteen years, said: "Ed is a visionary. He has these ideas and sometimes I think they are off-the-wall . . . but it's just his vision, his genius to see beyond mundane details" (*Arkansas Business,* April 29, 1985). Cromwell's critics and detractors may have been quick to call him a dreamer and to describe him as "a smart guy with no grasp of reality," but it was exactly Cromwell's ability to look past reality that helped the turnaround of downtown Little Rock which, in the '60s, resembled a large junkyard. In fact, public consensus was that downtown Little Rock, including the Capital Hotel, should be abandoned, leveled, dismantled, forgotten. Cromwell thought differently.

Ed Cromwell's Background

Edwin Boykin Cromwell was born on November 13, 1909, in the Philippines, specifically Manila, where his father, Ellis Cromwell, was collector of revenue for Philippine Islands under President William Howard Taft. Ellis and his wife, Ada Henley, were originally from Mississippi. Ed remembers that his family made the laborious, trans-oceanic journey back to the States several times—the entire trip taking more than six weeks to accomplish.

In 1912 Ellis died of a heart attack while hunting. Young Edwin and his mother returned to West Point, Mississippi, where he attended grade school and the first two years of high school. When he was fifteen, Cromwell left for boarding school; he attended and graduated from Mercersburg Academy in Mercersburg, Pennsylvania, in 1927.

From Mercersburg, Cromwell went to Princeton and graduated in 1931 with a bachelor's degree in architecture. He was accepted into the graduate program for architecture at Princeton and studied one year before coming to the realization that his chosen profession was being hard-hit by the Great Depression. Cromwell recalls looking for summer work at various architectural firms around the country (he traveled up and down the east coast). He would walk into these almost disserted, vacant offices; firms that had previously employed dozens if not hundreds of workers, were now empty and idle. It was not a good time to be an architect. To survive, Cromwell did construction work, painted signs, and cleaned bricks for five cents an hour.

Cromwell's Arrival in Little Rock

Cromwell put his dreams of becoming an architect on hold, left the East Coast and retreated to his home in West Point, Mississippi, where he taught high school mathematics for two years, earning $810 per year. In 1935 while in the nation's capital for a Princeton friend's wedding, Cromwell's passion was rekindled: "I wanted to get back in the flow of architecture. But if architecture was coming back, it wasn't coming back in a town of 6,000 [West Point]." While in Washington, Cromwell was able to land a job with the Federal Resettlement Administration. This federal agency was later to become the Farm Security Administration and was responsible for resettlement programs at Arkansas communities such as Lake Dick, Dyess, and Plum Bayou. Cromwell was assigned to an office in Little Rock, and he arrived in the city on December 6, 1935—just in time for Christmas holidays. "I fell in love with the city. I thought it was beautiful."

Cromwell stayed at the local YMCA for fifty cents a night. One of his friends introduced Cromwell to Henrietta Thompson, the daughter of local architect Charles L. Thompson. Ed and Henrietta would marry the next year, in 1937; their marriage lasted sixty-two years until her death in 1999. By coincidence, Ms. Thompson's great-grandfather was none other than Justice George C. Watkins who had sold the land to William B. Denckla back in 1872. Cromwell remembers one of the first social functions he attended was the gala debutante ball of Fanny Rose McGehee in the grand ballroom at the Capital Hotel. "The Capital was still in good condition then. Even then, I remember being impressed with the old hotel."

Because of a bureaucratic mix-up in his transfer paperwork, it took Cromwell over three months to get his first paycheck from the Resettlement Administration. While waiting for the bureaucratic wheels to churn, he found part-time employment as a night draftsman at several of the local architectural firms including Wittenberg and Delony where he eventually went to work full time. In 1941 he was offered a partnership with the architectural firm which had been Thompson, Sanders, and Ginnochio. Cromwell's father-in-law, Charles L. Thompson, had retired from the firm in 1938. Over the next fifty years, until his retirement in 1978, Cromwell would help build one of the leading architectural and engineering firms in the region.

A Career of Achievement

By 1974, Cromwell had several partners: Dietrich Neyland, John J. Truemper, Eugene P. Levy, and Oliver Gatchell. The name of the firm was Cromwell, Neyland, Truemper, Levy and Gatchell, Inc.

John Truemper's *A Century of Service,* published in 1985, chronicles some of the showcase projects and an array of architectural achievements. By then the firm had offices both in Little Rock and Memphis and had over 130 employees. While Cromwell's firm was regional, even national in scope, they had an impact locally and were responsible for such design projects as Winrock Farm, the Arkansas Arts Center, the Governor's Mansion, the UALR campus, the restoration of Villa Marre, Trapnall Hall, and last but not least, the Capital Hotel (John Truemper. *A Century of Service.* Little Rock: August House, 1985.)

Truemper notes that "The firm began to gain recognition not only locally but nationally as an important industrial design group. Projects which facilitated this recognition included plants for Warwick Electronics, Ameron Corporation's Enmar division, Teletype Corporation, ITT Continental Baking, Coca-Cola Bottling

Under Ed Cromwell's leadership, the Cromwell firm became one of the leading architectural and structural design engineering firms in the South. This photograph shows the part of the design area and architects at work in the late '70s. *(Cromwell Architects and Engineers, Inc.)*

Company, Yale and Towne, Emerson Electric, Firestone, Seiberling Rubber, Barrett Hamilton, Inc., Hoerner Box Company, Orbit Valve Company, Timex Corporation and Jacuzzi International" *(A Century of Service).*

Under Cromwell the firm broadened its capabilities into the fields of construction management, interior design, town and community planning, process engineering and design, real estate development, and historic preservation. Cromwell was the chief architect of Maumelle New Town.

Cromwell and his partners were closely tied to the Arkansas business community, and the gentleman architect's scope of civic duties expanded into a dizzy list of diverse activities.

Design Philosophy

From the beginning, Cromwell believed the starting point of any project was "to use a natural part of the land as the basis for design. The sensitivity to the natural environment is something we need to pay more attention to." With regard to Little Rock, Cromwell was acutely aware that the origin of the city had to do with the Arkansas River.

Cromwell also lamented the horrors of "urban sprawl"—the tendency of city dwellers to abandon downtown working areas in favor of cookie-cutter, suburban developments. Urban sprawl, Cromwell argued, cost people time and money. Urban sprawl was to architecture and housing what McDonald's was to the food industry. Furthermore, argued Cromwell, this kind of mass development left residents with little sense of history. "There's no there, there," says Cromwell, quoting Gertrude Stein. Instead of creating commuter communities outside the city, Cromwell wanted to renovate the grand old homes of downtown which, in the '60s, were being used as boardinghouses or flophouses. "I figured if you took the worst house in the neighborhood and made a financial commitment to it, it would pick up the neighborhood. So I bought two houses on Rock and Scott Streets" (*Arkansas Democrat*, October 30 1983).

Local banks were not accustomed to investing in dreams, and Cromwell said, "I had to make a personal commitment. I had to hock everything I had, but I was determined to set a standard. Not just a paint-up, fix up job, but the best of the old and the best of the new, such as new plumbing and wiring."

Cromwell's gamble paid off and his restoration work expanded. Eventually the Cromwell firm would be credited with the restoration of such historic buildings as Trapnell Hall, the Old Post Office and Customs House (University of Little Rock Law School), the Zeb Ward building, and over twenty residential projects in the Quapaw Quarter.

The Arkansas Territorial Restoration

For several decades, Cromwell served on the Board of the Arkansas Territorial Restoration Commission. His years of service reinforced Cromwell's historical perspective.

John L. Ferguson, state historian, says: "From 1821 to 1835 [when Arkansas became a state] the Territorial Legislature met in the Territorial Capital which continued to serve as a political gathering place until the Old State House was completed in 1839. In the 1930s, the Legislature created a commission to have charge of the project to restore the Old State House and appropriated funds to purchase the grounds and contribute to the restoration work; the Federal Government made it a WPA Project and contributed the labor. The Restoration was complete in the spring of 1941" ("Territorial Capitol Commission—General Plan of Grounds, Drawings and Brief History of Buildings").

According to Bill Worthen:

> Louise Loughborough was involved in the successful campaign to maintain state ownership of the Old State House after the General Assembly and other state offices left the building in 1912. In 1939 she led the campaign to save the half-block of houses, which became the Arkansas Territorial Restoration [now the Historic Arkansas Museum]. Initially she went to Floyd Sharp, the WPA administrator in Little Rock, to secure funding for the project. He politely dismissed her by saying he'd give her the money, but the property needed to be owned by a government entity. She then turned to the General Assembly, and, as Senator Ed Dillon explained it, she buttoned holed each legislator and read a 30 second statement of importance of restoring those structures. She was the "sweetest lady in the world," according to

Senator Dillon. She got her appropriation and returned to Mr. Sharp. Assuming his original dismissal had been permanent he had to be reminded of the project. "There was nothing I could do," said Sharp, but to gather resources from other projects and reallocate to this project in order to keep his promise. The Territorial Restoration was approved and on the way. It is clear that persuading Ed Cromwell to get involved in the museum was one of the savviest decisions she made for the Arkansas Territorial Restoration. His vision expanded the museum and led to its accreditation by the American Association of Museums.

(Note from Bill Worthen, dated September 7, 2001)

On the way to the Territorial Board meetings, Louise Loughborough and Cromwell would routinely walk by the aging Capital Hotel. Cromwell remembers that his preservationist mentor would always turn to him and say "Edwin, we must do something about the Capital Hotel."

Cromwell agreed.

Jim Pfeifer, Cromwell's Project Supervisor

Jim Pfeifer was Cromwell's project architect on the Capital Hotel. He also helped with a number of other Cromwellian restoration projects. A young man in his twenties at the time he worked with Cromwell, Pfeifer today looks a little like James Taylor: balding, thin, with angular facial features, a sensitive, soft-spoken man, introspective and intelligent. "I was born in Little Rock," says Pfeifer. " My great-grandfather had a boat store down the river. They would bring steamboats up, and he would sell different kinds of groceries and stuff to take up to plantations. I grew up here, went to school in upstate New York. My degree is a bachelor's degree in architecture from Cornell University. I'm a licensed architect. I first worked as a high-school student here at the Cromwell firm. I worked with Mr. Cromwell sometimes in the summer. I just worked for him privately, restoring houses in the Quapaw Quarter. That was probably my fondest experience. It was awesome, actually."

Pfeifer pauses, looks wistfully in the distance.

> I would go out and measure up buildings, and he would say, "Take this over to the bank and see if you can sell it." I would say, "What?!" They [the banks] laughed at Mr. Cromwell. He had always been respected as a businessman and head of a big firm. But this preservation stuff, a lot of people laughed at him. You know, it was the 1950s, '60s. These old buildings, they wanted to knock them down, like the Marion. They just wanted to wipe them away.

Again a pause and a wistful look.

> So, I would measure up a lot of buildings, and he would try to get banks interested in them, and he was successful. He did some of the first, I suppose you would call them "Gentrified" restorations. Basically, they were buildings that people didn't care much about, even though they were managing and living in them. He restored the exteriors and put in some handsome interior apartments, but still maintained the look of a single-family old mansion. I kind of just followed him through the years in all of this, and I had the oppor-

tunity to work with him and around him and just be a friend. I could show you a building down the street here, 1880s or 1870s on Markham, that is sitting there now . . . I remember Mr. Cromwell came to work one day, and he saw a wrecker and a bulldozer—you know, kind of mobilizing next to it. He knows the owner, a guy named Alexander. So he calls Mr. Alexander and asks him what the bulldozer is doing there. He said, "Aw hell, I am tired of paying the insurance on the thing, I'm tearing it down."

Cromwell said "I tell you what, if I pay your next insurance premium and pay off the demolition guy for whatever he's spent this morning, can you hold off for a while and let me see if I can do something with this building?" No one really knows all this. I mean, he saved the building. That's the way he operated. The building doesn't really have a name. It's on the corner of Markham and Chester. It s a beautiful two-story brick building on the southwest corner of Markham and Chester. He did this thing from his soul.

Another building I remember was a flophouse. He bought it from some investors and got the financing together and restored it into some really nice apartments. It had a central hall with a grand round stairway in it. They built four apartments in it. They were beautiful, and they maintained the central stairs and exteriors and so forth. There was this old lady, I'll call her Miss Kate. She didn't own the building, but she was allowed to live there for years, with little or no rent because she collected rent from some rough characters. If they didn't pay, she'd kick them out; she was a tough old gal. She lived in the front bedroom and had a little kitchenette and bathroom . . . one room really. When the renovation started, she was obviously concerned that she would lose her home. She was elderly, and Mr. Cromwell, against the advice of some of the investors, left her there. He remodeled the whole house around her. He kept Miss Kate in her home which had some sliding doors at the front. I remember Miss Kate would open up the sliding doors and peek out while the construction going on. The whole house was almost gutted.

Cromwell built Miss Kate a modern bathroom and kitchen. I was off at college then, and when I came back to see if she was still living there, she still had those sliding doors. By then the apartments were finished and rented to young lawyers and advertising executive types. She would say to me, "Jim, you wouldn't believe the kind of money these folks are paying for these apartments. They're really nice." Sure Cromwell was a businessman, but he also worked from his heart and soul.

Little Rock's Downtown Wasteland, 1965–1977

Another of Cromwell's recruits and devoted followers was a young man named Larry Martin. Today Martin lives in New Mexico and runs a successful marketing and business development company. Martin worked for Cromwell and eventually founded the Quapaw Real Estate Firm with Tom Wilkes.

"I grew up here," says Martin. "I went to school in North Little Rock, then went to Hendrix College. I studied literature and philosophy and was going to get a double major. But, it is a small school, and I didn't really like the head of the department so I switched to physics and got my degree in physics for no particularly good reason. And then I went to California and worked in television for several years." Life in California wasn't all that it was cracked up to be; Martin returned to Little Rock and went to work for Ed Cromwell in 1967.

At that time the architect had his offices on Spring Street. Martin was hired to do marketing and business development, rather an unusual position for an architectural and engineering firm. "I reported to Ed because nobody else really knew what a marketing guy was supposed to do. Frankly, neither did I."

Martin was soon to find out: his first assignment was to photo document most of downtown Little Rock. "I never paid any attention to architecture or urban planning . . . I was really very fortunate to get the opportunity to get to know and work with Ed. He is a visionary . . . and he never met a challenge that he didn't want to overcome."

Martin soon discovered that what Cromwell had in mind was a revitalization of downtown: "His ideas and vision were written off as daydreaming by some city planners and politicians. They had their own plans."

Critics of Cromwell weren't just being party poopers. There was some good reason for their skepticism. On January 17, 1971 the *Arkansas Democrat* ran a story entitled "Our River—The Central Theme in an Architect's Vision of an Aesthetic City":

> Significant voices in Little Rock are telling the city to return to the river . . . the object of Little Rock's dream—the healing or circumvention of all the ills that plague urban American growth—is right where it was when Bernard de la Harpe stepped off the boat at "la petite roche"—the little rock—in 1722.
>
> Yet there is irony here.
>
> Could he return, La Harpe might have a hard time finding his petite roche. In 1971, two and a half centuries later, the spot is practically inaccessible. To get to it, one has to cross a maze of mud and railroad tracks, skirt a scrap metal reclamation plant, climb over a wire fence, and descend con-

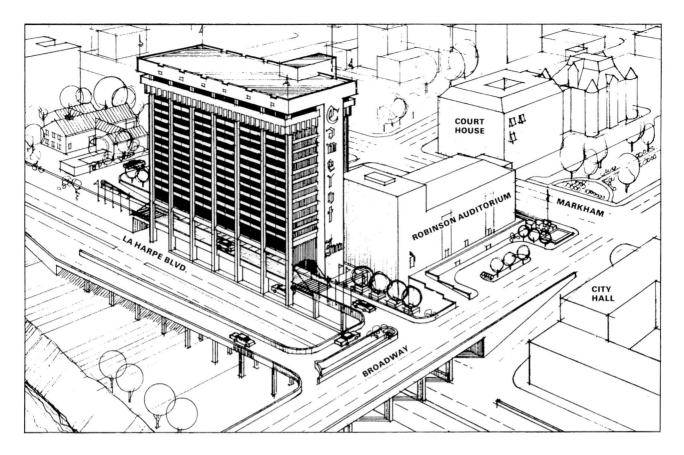

Drawing of proposed
Convention Center.
*(Little Rock Chamber of
Commerce)*

crete steps to the front of a huge steel-girded bridge on which a sign reads:
"Danger—Blasting Beyond This Point."

But for fear of weeping, La Harpe might laugh.

Actually, the inaccessibility of La Harpe's rock merely signifies a deeper
and sadder problem—the fact that, until recently—Little Rock has literally
turned its back on the stream that spawned its infancy and has abandoned
the Arkansas River. At some point it was transmuted to become . . . a place
where errant teen-agers and young adults went on Saturday nights to drink
beer and do other wicked things.

Late in the article, Cromwell is quoted:

"It's a hell of a note that we've built our cities so that we can hardly wait
to get away from them." He [Cromwell] wants Little Rock to stop fleeing
and ultimately to sit down with itself, to consider its long history and unique
geographical setting and then plan a city that is more than a hodge-podge of
errant commercial or cultural developments. Not content just to clean up
the area around the river, Cromwell drew grand analogies to other historic
cities around the globe: . . . If that project is pursued—Cromwell argues—
then the Arkansas will not only become 'our river' again, it will also become
the nucleus of the city's being, a place where people live and work and play
in that idyllic mood which draws Londoners to the Thames, Romans to St.
Peter's Square and Venetians to St. Marks . . . The city, Cromwell argues,
must be a mosaic of "great spaces where people love to be." He speaks enthusiastically about the citizenry's "spiritual response to places," and he speaks

Ed Cromwell, in 1971 as he discusses the importance of the Arkansas River in the founding of the city of Little Rock. During the '60s and '70s, Cromwell campaigned to save many of Little Rock's historic structures during an era when most people favored urban renewal and demolition of buildings such as the Grady Manning Hotel. (Arkansas Democrat-Gazette)

disparagingly about "visual pollution." The idea that Little Rock might rank up there with London and St. Peter's Square seems a bit of a stretch, but such hyperbole was perhaps needed to get people's attention, to counter the existing apathy and get the idea of redevelopment of downtown on the public radar screen. Little Rock, claimed Cromwell, "still retains some of the finest architectural features in the country." Among them, Cromwell cited: the State Capital, the old Pulaski County Courthouse, Robinson Auditorium, the Old State House, the restored Territorial Capitol, the Capital Hotel, and a host of other 19th century dwellings.

There were a few other public officials who supported, at least in part, Cromwell's vision. These included Doyle Rogers, the commercial real estate developer, and Don Venhaus, Little Rock's director of community development who pointed out, "The dream can be realized when the public has the wherewithal to do it with. At present state law imposes a 5-mill ceiling on taxes a city may approve for capital improvements. That ceiling has already been reached and revenue has already been pledged to other projects."

Dreams are free; buildings, renovation, and public works along the lines that Cromwell was suggesting had a price tag. The city had a budget, and there was no cash to fund either works of faith or dreams, no matter how worthy or well intentioned.

Larry Martin noted that "It took a lot of imagination to project and envision the potential of downtown. Robinson Auditorium was basically abandoned. In fact that entire part of the city was so far abandoned at the time; nobody really could imagine anybody wanting to come there. Walking the streets in that area felt very dangerous at the time."

The Capital Hotel under the Cassinelli sisters was in its mid-to-late brothel period: rooms by the hour. There was also a billiard hall on the ground floor of the hotel. "Guests" from out of state arrived at the adjacent bus station: a sort of mecca for bums, thieves, prostitutes, and other unsavory types. The Marion and the Grady Manning Hotels were semi-abandoned, as was a five-story parking lot.

The "out of town tourists," as Elizabeth Cassinelli described them, would arrive by the busload. After playing a little pool and finding some cheap wine, guests from the bus station would make their way to another nearby building where the room rate was just right—free. This happened to be the Tannenbaum Cold Storage Plant which Cromwell, as part of his crusade was trying to save. "It was an interesting building and I thought its design and placement next to the river had some historical value," said Cromwell.

The Tannenbaum was an abandoned multi-level warehouse situated by the river where the outdoor amphitheater would eventually be built. It had a low-rise portion and a five-story cork-insulated, tower with no windows. It was just a big block of a thing that stood up.

The Tannenbaum turned out to be a real Mecca for the bums and thieves. The cork-insulated rooms were cool in the heat of the summer and warm in the winter. It was a great place to gather, gamble, drink, sleep, and cheat your life away. A transient group of professional bums and assorted underworld characters would get drunk and set fires built from pieces of the building.

On one of his tours of the Tannenbaum with Cromwell, Scott Martin, a structural engineer at the architect's firm, remembers, "When you walked through the building, there were clothes stacked about two feet thick all across the floor." Although unlaundered and perhaps a little moldy and rotten, one could always be sure of finding additional evening attire at the beloved Tannenbaum.

One night the celebration inside the old warehouse evidently got a little too festive and out of hand: a fire started that destroyed most of the facility. That part of Cromwell's dream died. Downtown Little Rock by the river was a wasteland.

Turning the Dream into Reality

One of Cromwell's clients who eventually came to see the possibilities of a revitalized downtown was William S. Mitchell, then president of the Arkansas Bar Association. Mitchell had hired Cromwell to design an office library. At the time, the ABA was housed in a little white, five-thousand-square-foot building near the first State Capital. The ABA wanted an appropriate new building, one with a library.

A counter-Cromwell faction that had political clout was the Southwest Hotel Corporation, a Texas-based hotel chain firm that had a lock on what remained of the hotel business downtown including the Grady Manning and Marion Hotels. Southwest had their own ideas for development—one that would not compete with their existing hotel properties. Southwest, along with city planners looked away from the river towards sites on Main Street between Second and Third.

By the mid-'60s the Marion was being used in part as a residence hotel. The hotel's bar—the Gar Hole—had once been a place for legislators to meet, but the focus of political and business activity had shifted when Witt Stephens built the Coachman's Inn.

Young, naive and unaware of the unlikely success of the project or the enormity of the political hurdles to be overcome, Larry Martin continued his photo

documentation of the area all around Robinson Auditorium, down to the state-house and the river. "I took various kinds of views from various vantage points, and then Ed had some of the firm architects do some sketches of what the potential of the area could be; we put together a slide show. At the request of Little Rock mayor Martin Borchett, the Cromwell firm built a model of a proposed convention center and adjacent buildings."

Cromwell's vision had taken shape. The model was about four feet square; it included the Robinson Auditorium and the State House and the Arkansas River at one end of it, the courthouse and the new hotels and convention site at the other end.

The slide show and model did help Cromwell to persuade Mitchell and the ABA to postpone their building project; he promised that their patience would allow for a more coordinated development of the area.

Larry Martin said, "Ed kept telling the folks at the Bar Association that it was important to be visionary; he told them to think about the importance of their site and its location on the riverfront and adjoining the Robinson Auditorium and what it would mean to the city."

Cromwell, the slide show, and the model circulated. Cromwell argued that the proposed convention center site would reconnect Little Rock with the river. The vision was a hard sell.

Besides Cromwell, the Chamber of Commerce, and Fifty for the Future, a group of business and civic leaders who took on such projects as the development of the Jacksonville Air Force Base, were actively seeking alternative plans. "Fifty for the Future paid for a feasibility study to determine if the Hilton Hotel chain would locate in the city several years ago. The study was forwarded to the Hilton chain, but nothing ever came of it" (*Arkansas Democrat,* September 6, 1970).

At the same time Hilton was being wined and dined, Cromwell's model made the rounds of various public venues. It was in all the bank lobbies. Once or twice the model got lost or ended up in storage closets—an apt symbol of the entire project. Finally the model ended up in the break room of the Chamber of Commerce where it was displayed like a corpse; businessmen and employees filing past it, drinking sodas and coffee.

One day Cromwell got a call from George Miller, who was then executive director of Fifty for the Future. Miller called Cromwell: "Ed, we've got a fellow who wants to talk to you about this model."

Abe Hester was a hotel developer from Tulsa who had come to Little Rock in search of a new hotel site. After a day with the chamber people and tours around the city he had given up. While waiting for his plane back to Tulsa, Hester ended up in the chamber break room for a cup of coffee. That's when he saw the Cromwell model.

Opposite and above: Downtown Little Rock in 1970 was mixture of abandoned warehouses, half-demolished buildings, rubble, and trash along the railroad tracks. Buildings such as the abandoned Tannenbaum warehouse provided a mecca for unsavory characters who also frequented the billiard hall and liquor store at the Capital Hotel. Ed Cromwell wanted Little Rock to revitalize the area along the Arkansas River, which had provided the foundation for the original trading post established by French explorer La Harpe. Cromwell was a sole voice among architects and city planners who wanted most buildings, including the Capital, leveled. (Arkansas Democrat-Gazette)

Hester wanted to build a hotel that would be part of a new convention facility. Early that day he had been lobbied by city planners on the Main Street location, but they had not shown him Cromwell's concept.

"That's what I want." said Hester upon seeing the model. Cromwell had at last found an out-of-state-disciple.

On September 1, 1970, the Chamber of Commerce made the announcement of the new project in its weekly newsletter: "New $8 Million Convention Complex Planned: Camelot Hotel Linked to Robinson Auditorium—Project to Include Underground Garage, Plaza and Bar Center":

> Plans were announced on September 5, for a proposed $8,000,000 Convention Center Hotel Complex in downtown Little Rock. The project would involve construction of a 310-room convention hotel containing an 800-seat banquet hall; extensive renovation of Robinson Memorial Auditorium, to be physically linked with the new hotel; construction of a 565-car underground parking garage; development of a landscaped pedestrian Plaza area and a headquarters facility for the Arkansas Bar Association. The area involved in the sizable development is located between Conway Street at the Old State House and Robinson Auditorium at Markham and Broadway.
>
> In a news conference held at the Little Rock Club, officials of Fifty for the Future, Inc., and the Little Rock Chamber of Commerce disclosed that the Kin-Ark Corporation of Tulsa, Oklahoma proposes to construct a $4,600,000 hotel adjacent to the auditorium. The firm, which owns the Camelot Inn at Tulsa, will finance the facility through a $3,500,000 mortgage, sale of $600,000 in convertible debenture bonds and $500,000 in equity money provided by Kin-Ark. Permanent mortgage money will be provided by a combination of all Pulaski County banks, savings and loan associations and home-owned life insurance companies.
>
> The Northeast corner of the Plaza will be the location of the Bar Association Center. The $250,000 Center will contain the State Offices of the Arkansas Bar Association, a library, reception and seminar rooms contained within a 12,000 sq. ft. building. The Center's architecture will be designed to harmonize with the Old State House and Robinson Auditorium.
>
> W. F. Rector, who succeeded George Miller, President of Fifty for the Future, Inc., stated the entire Convention Center Complex proposal "represents the combined efforts of many people and organizations who have worked together in an effort to make the proposal a reality."
>
> Werner C. Knoop, president of the Chamber of Commerce, noted that the organization has placed "major emphasis" in 1970 to "acquire modern and adequate meeting and lodging facilities to serve the convention needs of Little Rock now and in the future."
>
> Howard K. Edwards, president of Kin-Ark Corporation, expressed his organization's appreciation for the cooperation of the many agencies and individuals involved in the multi-million dollar project.

A few days later the *Arkansas Gazette* urged that "West Markham Should Be Widened" to accommodate the additional traffic which would be generated by the new convention center. "West Markham has suffered decline through the years, and the closing of the Hotel Marion was a misfortune for the old street. Greater width should bring new buildings, new activities and greatly increased property values. But we should not wait today for the slow operation of a setback plan. Surgery is needed. The job would be easier now than it would have been in years past. The Marion Hotel would have been a formidable obstacle, but it is no longer a business. The Grady Manning Hotel would be an obstacle and so might that old Grand Dame of hostelries, the historic Capital Hotel" (*Arkansas Gazette,* September 14, 1970).

Demolition and urban "surgery" not preservation and restoration were the catch phrases of the day.

Doyle Rogers

Public support and funding were difficult to come by, and while the Kin-Ark's Camelot was eventually built, it was not until 1978 that a finance package was finally approved for the Excelsior and Convention Center. A key figure in the final stages of the convention center development was Doyle Rogers, a commercial real-estate magnate who, among other projects, had constructed the Colony West Shopping Center in West Little Rock.

Rogers had a friend who had been involved with the construction of the Miami convention center in which Hyatt Hotels had been a partner. A similar proposal to Hyatt and a number of other hotel chains failed to get attention, so Rogers stepped

Grady Manning and Capital Hotels prior to 1980. *(Cromwell Architects and Engineers, Inc.)*

up to the plate. He was able to negotiate the purchase of key riverfront properties including the old Marion and Grady Manning Hotels from Southwest. Secondly, he offered to build and partially fund the Excelsior Hotel.

The convention center finance package was eventually approved, and with much fanfare and attention the Grady Manning and Marion Hotels were imploded. Construction started on the Excelsior in 1980, which opened in 1982.

The efforts of Doyle Rogers and those associated with the Convention Center were key to the revitalization of downtown which in turn made it possible for Ed Cromwell to attract financing for the beloved Capital Hotel.

CHAPTER THREE

THE MIRACLE ON MARKHAM STREET

THE MIRACLE ON MARKHAM STREET, PART ONE

Early Negotiations with the Cassinelli Family

In 1972, activity in and around what was to become the Little Rock Convention Center prompted Cromwell to rent an office in the Capital Hotel. The company set up shop in what is now the Capital Bar. It served as a good vantage point and base of operations for the firm. The condition of the Capital by then was in rapid decline. The stained-glass window in the lobby ceiling looked as if it might fall out any minute. There were broken and lose tiles in the floor downstairs. The beautiful ionic columns were in very bad shape. The roof was leaking frequently.

Amelia Cassinelli continued to accept what business she could, holding fast to the dream that one day, somehow, some way, that things would be different. The billiard parlor on the ground floor lobby was still open, and the assorted crowd of transients and prostitutes would mingle and maraud round the neighborhood after dark.

During this period Cromwell remembers that Amelia was interested in the idea of selling the property; her health, like the very building she managed, was failing. Among other problems, she developed a kidney ailment. Her health issues added new urgency to the negotiations; nevertheless, Amelia was firm about the asking price of $500,000 or more.

Cromwell was not the only one interested in the Capital. The owners of the adjacent bus station desperately needed additional parking; they were interested in tearing down the Capital and using the land to build a parking deck. In spite of the financial allure, the Cassinellis really didn't want their hotel torn down: "We owe them a great deal of appreciation because they did under great odds save the Capital," said Cromwell. "Several times during the seventies I made offers to ask for options and they wouldn't give options. Amelia was a pretty strong business-woman and she said 'no options,' take my price or leave it."

Undaunted by Amelia's stubbornness, Cromwell commissioned a number of feasibility studies to determine alternative uses for the property. One of the proposals was to turn the hotel into an office building, since one of the drawbacks of the Capital was its limited number of rooms, making it commercially unviable. Projections and existing hotel management models proved that if the Capital was to be run as a hotel and be profitable, additional rooms would have to be built. An addition would have to be made—not as part of the existing structure, but on the back lot behind the hotel which at the time was owned by Commercial National Bank. The bank owned and operated a drive-in bank there at that time.

Larry Martin wrote Cromwell the following memo on June 20, 1974:

> This is to bring you up to date on our studies for revitalizing the Capital Hotel.
>
> About a year ago we looked at the possibility of converting the structure for office use, saving the major public spaces and restoring the exterior. Ollie Gatchell investigated the structure of the building and determined that it would require substantial renovation to support office floor load requirements. Based on his recommendations, we had some preliminary drawings made and did a cost estimate with the help of Baldwin Company. The cost of rebuilding the structure for office use, while preserving its historic character, proved too high to make it feasible, so we took a look at other possible uses.
>
> Ollie tells us that the structure is adequate for residential uses provided it is sprinkled for fire protection. With this in mind we began exploring the possibility of restoring the hotel to its original condition and operating it as a first quality hotel with a unique historic flair.
>
> Not being knowledgeable hotel operators, we looked first for an experienced consultant who could tell us if this approach would be realistic, or if we were just barking up a tree. Your friend Leslie Moore of Corrigan Hotels recommended we get in touch with C. DeWitt ("Witt") Coffman of Coral Gables, Florida. Witt has managed over 100 hotels and now operates as a management and marketing consultant for new hotels and for older ones which are having troubles . . . Witt recommends that we consider purchasing the southwest quarter of the block from Commercial National Bank, along with the hotel, to provide parking and expansion room. Our conversation with Dick Butler indicated that the bank is now in a position to sell the property . . . We have remained in constant contact with Amelia Cassinelli, and come to an agreement on a purchase price of $550,000 for the hotel including all appurtenances . . . We are estimating the price of the Commercial National Bank property at $250,000 . . . the cost of rejuvenation and expansion depends upon Witt's recommendations concerning construction of new rooms, which we should have in hand within a week . . . he is looking at a minimum of just restoring the existing building and a maximum of adding 100 rooms in a new wing.

Cromwell was also thinking that the hotel needed to be restored. Among his personal files are notes on added "attractions" that could bring additional interest and business to the hotel.

> Have family style restaurant: possum. Spoon bread. Greens. Duck. Wild Razorback. Squirrel Mulligan Stew. Catfish. Beer. Hush puppies. Run a horse drawn carriage to the train station and back. Maybe form a condominium rental pool. Corporations, legislators, politicians, etc. make it extremely fancy. Get Rotary Club in; they don't have a big enough place to meet. Kiwanis second. Capital would be dependent on convention overflows. Scads of small sales conferences going on.

The Placing of the Capital on the National Register of Historic Places

To combat the possibility that the Capital might be torn down, Cromwell and others pushed to get the building placed on the National Register of Historic Places. On March 8, 1974, William E. Henderson, the State Preservation Officer, submitted an application; Diana Kirk was the research historian. An excerpt from the application reads as follows:

> This excellent example of Victorian grandeur boasts seventeen bays across its façade. Projecting from the front elevation is a one-story portico five bays in length and supported by six columns with Corinthian capitals. The second-story porch deck is enclosed by a simple wrought iron railing, and surrounded by a canopy edged with decorative iron scroll work . . . Across the entire length of the first story front elevation has engaged Corinthian columns between each bay. With the exception of the deck projection on the second floor, the second and third story façades are identical with the two, semi-elliptical headed windows separated by squared columns. The fourth story, added about 1889, has a mullion window with transom between each Corinthian capitalized pilaster.
>
> On entering the main lobby of the Capital Hotel, one first notices the inlaid tile flooring, the two parallel rows of columns with uniquely decorated capitals, and the gray marble staircase located opposite the entrance. Both squared marble and round painted columns support the exposed beams which terminate in a recessed ceiling. Thick panels of highly polished gray marble line the interior walls of the lobby. On the west side is the hotel desk with the original wrought iron grill work and etched glass panels.

The application was reviewed and approved. In 1977 the Capital was placed on the National Register, a significant event that insured the building's future, in some form.

Amelia's Death and Cromwell's Initial Investor Group.

Amelia Cassinelli's declining health worsened, and in 1976 she passed away from complications due to kidney failure. Almost immediately, Elizabeth made the decision that she wanted to sell the Capital at a reduced price to Cromwell who had scrambled to put together an investment-management team. Larry Martin recalls, "Ed asked me to help put together a financial analysis because I was doing that kind of work at the time. The people in the first management group had a lot of heart but no experience running a hotel and no specific knowledge of what it takes to put a deal like this together. We weren't able to catch anybody's attention . . . it was going to take many millions of dollars to do this project, and it was at a time when people didn't think the hotel business was worth investing a lot of money in anyway."

Among those in Cromwell's initial investor group were Shelby Blackmon, one-time city attorney; Wernor Knoop; Art Pfeifer; Jack Frost; Gaines Norton; Carl Miller Jr. Also serving on the initial board were Watt Gregory, George Pitts, Ray Cannon, and Olin Wright. Investors chipped in ten thousand dollars apiece, and enough money was raised to consummate a buyer-seller agreement with Elizabeth. The group paid for the board-up of the hotel and the removal for safe-keeping and storage of stained glass, light fixtures, and assorted hardware from the 1908 remodeling.

In a grant application to the Arkansas Historic Preservation Committee, Cromwell would later write,

> . . . each day the hotel lies abandoned, the risk of fire and vandalism is substantial. The Hotel has been vandalized several times this year despite efforts to make it secure. The proposed convention center will be enhanced by the proximity of a historic, luxury hotel. Metro Center mall will likewise be accessible to patrons of the new Capital Hotel.

With the property now in hand, Cromwell began an intensive and increasingly frustrating search for investors. At the time their budget was about $4 million to renovate the hotel.

On May 24, 1977, Cromwell mailed out a survey to almost every business leader in town.

> The question before us is whether such an excellent facility [the Capital] will be used. You will make a difference, and your opinions and ideas are needed . . . The Capital can be an outstanding hospitality institution in the mid-south, a delightful place to eat, sleep, conduct business or relax and enjoy oneself. Room rates are projected to begin as low as $24 . . .

Response to the survey and interest in the Capital was very positive, but getting people to step forward and to commit $4 million was not to be. Among those on Cromwell's initial investor hit list was Witt Stephens. "I remember him looking at me with his feet up on his desk, smoking a cigar like he always did," says Cromwell. "He was supportive of the idea but as a business deal Witt wasn't interested unless Charlie Murphy in El Dorado would also be a partner. I went to see Murphy. He wasn't interested, and that was that. Stephens didn't get involved at that point." Witt Stephens had built and was still operating the Coachmen's Inn which had become Little Rock's political and business hub. Stephens had passed on the deal, and so Cromwell continued his search for funding.

Typical of the sort of feelers and contacts that were made was a December 12, 1977, memo from Cromwell to the group:

> As a result of a contact with John O'Brian, Vice President, Marriott for U.S. Development, we have had talks with Arthur Duggan, President, Inn America, Inc., of Boston. Arthur has been in the hotel business 16 years, owns several and manages several hotels, including 7 or 8 Sheratons and some small inns in Massachusetts. He might be interested in making a proposal to the Capital Hotel Group. Would like to meet with our "principals." Therefore we are planning a working lunch here at One Spring street at 12:15, Wednesday, December 14. Hope you will come.

The letters, phone calls, and fax campaign continued, but investors weren't interested.

Structural brainstorming on the Capital also continued. Larry Martin said,

"There were many plans floated and talked about. There was even discussion of taking out the main stairs and adding some rooms. The basic problem was how to get enough revenue out of a building like this to pay for the proportion of public space, common areas, and non-revenue spaces."

Dietrich Neyland, Cromwell's partner was instrumental in coming up with a design that included tearing down the two wings added on the south of the hotel and building an eight story tower which would enable the hotel to accommodate up to 150 rooms. Other hotel consultants suggested adding a swimming pool and a seventies style, *Saturday Night Fever*–type discothèque lounge.

The condition of the Capital worsened almost daily. Jim Pfeifer, Cromwell's project engineer, tells a story that captures the conditions at the time:

> One of my most vivid memories was when Mr. Cromwell was out there trying to find financing. Leventhal and Horowitz had their top guns coming in and a big chunk of the financing depended on them signing-off on it. They do feasibility studies for project financing. It was very important that they signed off on the project. Mr. Cromwell tells me, "I'm on my way out of town but these people are coming into town from Leventhal and Horowitz and you need to show them around the hotel and sell it to them!" I was young enough to kind of think, "Oh my gosh, what has he got me into?" So here I am, fairly inexperienced, willing and excited about the project, and these high-powered folks come into town. So I take them over there and it's raining . . . really pouring. The immediate neighborhood was in shambles. They had just demolished the Marion. Then there was the pool hall on the lobby level of the Capital. Next to that is the bus station with all kinds of folks kind of milling around out there, and around the corner is Max's Pawn Shop. So there is this padlock on a chain around the door, I open it up, throw open the doors to the hotel. Water is pouring down through the roof. It is about three inches deep in the lobby of the hotel. The previous winter it froze and part of the tile was heaved up, the plaster was falling down in the hotel and I'm supposed to sell this?

Leventhal and Horowitz would eventually see Cromwell's vision, but the struggle to find initial financing continued with yet more letters and phone calls. Through a contact made by Anne Bartley, Aetna Life and Casualty Company was targeted as a potential corporate investor. Bartley held the post of director of the Department of Arkansas Natural Cultural Heritage. In a letter to Donald Conrad—executive vice president of Aetna, dated January 24, 1978, Bartley wrote

> Everyone from the Governor to Senator Bumpers, the Mayor of Little Rock, history buffs, and just interested citizens have written that they want to see it [the Capital] renovated and they would use it . . . I do hope that financing the renovation of the Capital Hotel fits in with your Corporate Responsibilities Program. Not only as the State Historic Preservation Officer for Arkansas, but also as a person vitally interested in downtown Little Rock, I know that the reopening of the Capital Hotel would make a significant and positive impact on downtown Little Rock.

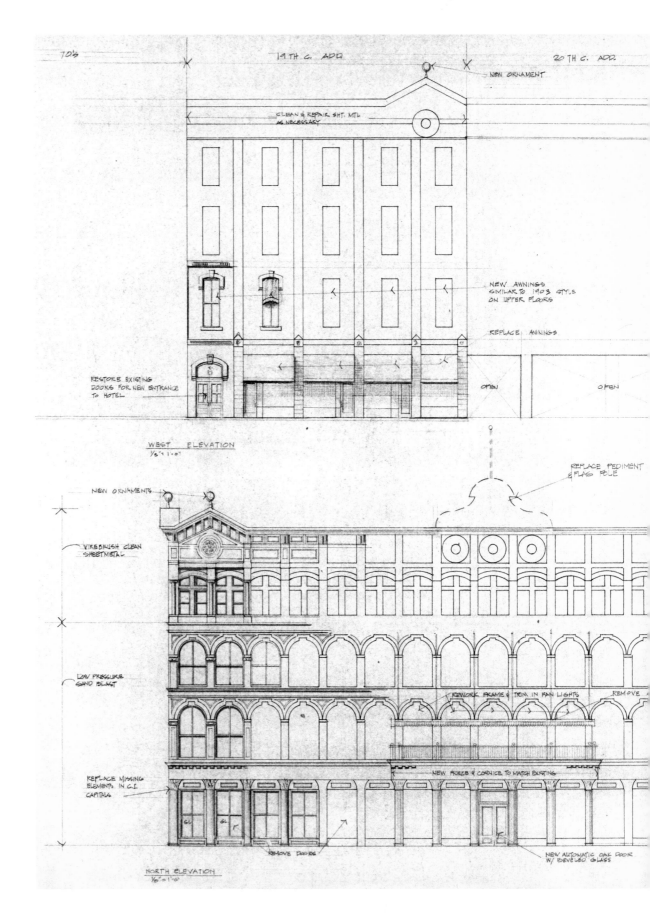

70'S   19TH C. ADD.   20TH C. ADD.

NEW ORNAMENT

CLEAN & REPAIR SHT. MTL. AS NECESSARY

NEW AWNINGS SIMILAR TO 1903 STYLE ON UPPER FLOORS

REPLACE AWNINGS

RESTORE EXISTING DOORS FOR NEW ENTRANCE TO HOTEL

OPEN   OPEN

WEST ELEVATION
1/8" = 1'-0"

REPLACE PEDIMENT & FLAG POLE

NEW ORNAMENTS

WIREBRUSH CLEAN SHEETMETAL

LOW PRESSURE SAND BLAST

REWORK FRAME & TRIM IN FAN LIGHTS   REMOVE

NEW FRIEZE & CORNICE TO MATCH EXISTING

REPLACE MISSING ELEMENTS IN C.I. CAPITALS

REMOVE DOORS

NEW AUTOMATIC OAK DOOR W/ BEVELED GLASS

NORTH ELEVATION
1/8" = 1'-0"

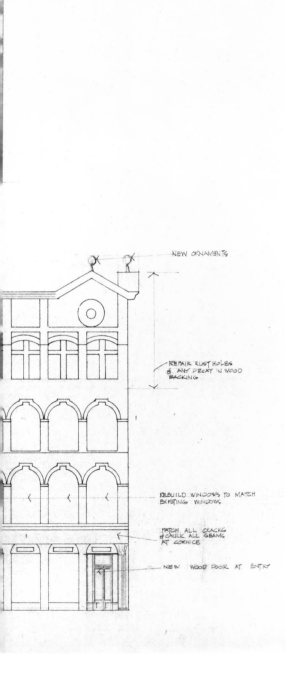

NEW ORNAMENTS

REPAIR RUST HOLES
& ANY DECAY IN WOOD
BACKING

REBUILD WINDOWS TO MATCH
EXISTING WINDOWS

PATCH ALL CRACKS
& CAULK ALL SEAMS
AT CORNICE

NEW WOOD DOOR AT ENTRY

Many plans for refurbishing and expanding the Capital were talked about. For example, Dietrich Neyland, Cromwell's partner, came up with a design that included tearing down the two wings added on the south of the hotel and building an eight-story tower which would enable the hotel to accommodate up to 150 rooms. Other hotel consultants suggested adding a swimming pool and a '70s-style, *Saturday Night Fever*–type discothèque lounge. At last it was decided to keep the original design of the building and to construct an addition to the back. These design sketches and notes show some of the restoration details which were planned, including such details as wire brushing the sheet metal on the sheet-metal façade of the fourth floor.

Right and opposite: These two photographs show the condition of the outside of the Capital Hotel prior to restoration work begun in 1980. (*Cromwell Architects and Engineers, Inc.*)

The Formation of a New Investor Group

Aetna was not interested. Time and money had run out for Cromwell's group. Part of the problem was that money was tight: interest rates were pushing 20 percent and other construction projects were at a standstill nationwide and locally. Cromwell remembered: "Twenty-two percent was a standard mortgage rate at the time; it made developing and building almost impossible. So we cashed in and tried to pay our debts and that was it."

The group met with Elizabeth Cassinelli and her attorney to inform them that they had been unable to secure financing and would have to hand the Capital back over to Elizabeth who promptly burst into tears: "I don't want the hotel back," she said. Elizabeth's attorney argued that under terms of the contract the group was still obligated to the project. Cromwell agreed to continue to try and find financing. Shelby Blackmon, former city attorney and part of the original investor group, suggested that the group "go out and sell to each county in the state a certain room and let each county own that room and furnish it." "It was a weird concept," said Cromwell, "and I wasn't interested in that at all. I said I'm going my way and you go yours and let's see who can do it."

A turning point for Cromwell was the work that Doyle Rogers was doing. Funding and plans for the Convention Center and Excelsior Hotel were approved, and with this, the business community started to believe in the vision of a revitalized downtown.

Cromwell's initial investor group was dissolved, but almost immediately he

Right and opposite: The Marion Hotel, was designed by architect George R. Mann who moved to Little Rock from Missouri in 1900. Mann also designed the Arkansas Gazette and Donaghey Buildings and the Pulaski County Courthouse, and he also provided H. F. Auten with the alterations for the Capital Hotel including storefronts, and the lobby. The newer Marion overshadowed the Capital to some extent; it was a much larger hotel with 175 rooms, lavish parlors, and an ornamental lobby and ballroom. In 1980, the Marion was imploded to make room for the new Excelsior Hotel and the Convention Center. (Arkansas Democrat-Gazette)

attracted two new key new players: Charles Bland, a businessman from Tennessee, and Lawrence Walters of Little Rock. These two men joined Cromwell's company, Historic Ventures. The partnership was announced in the *Democrat* in 1978:

The Capital Hotel Partnership
New Owners to restore Historic Old Capital Hotel

The historic Capital Hotel, located at the southwest corner of Markham and Louisiana Streets, is under new ownership and plans are in the works to restore the deluxe 98-room hotel.

The new Capital Hotel owners, Charles Bland, Jr. of Grand Junction, Tennessee; Lawrence E. Walters of Little Rock, and Historic Ventures Inc. of

Little Rock, plan a $4 million renovation to get underway the first of next year.

Architect Ed Cromwell, the president of Historic Ventures, had a purchase agreement for the hotel over a year and has previously announced his hopes to renovate it.

Bland has had 20-years experience in developing and constructing over 500 hotels worldwide. He is former managing director of Holiday Inn International. Walters said his most recent experience was the renovation and remodeling of a palace in Peru into a 130 room Marriott Hotel.

(*Arkansas Democrat,* October 31, 1978)

In an interview, Cromwell added the following details and insights to the story:

For the next two or three years—1978–1980—I worked very diligently to find developers. I went all over the country and traveled a great deal. In 1980, things really started to happen. Miracle after miracle happened, and the pieces all came together.

First of all, there was a fellow named Mack Hogue who was a partner with a big developer in Dallas, and he had built the Tower building with Win Rockefeller. He was Win's partner in that, and of course we had done a lot of work for Win who made the introduction. As it turns out, Mack was also starting up a new hotel chain called the Lincoln Hotels in Dallas; they were going to build a chain of hotels from California to New York, about fifteen to twenty hotels, top-flight hotels; similar to the Four Seasons. Lincoln was just getting started, and I think they had one or two hotels at that time, including one in Nashville called the Vanderbilt.

Anyway, some top execs from Lincoln came and looked over the Capital Hotel. They told me they would be interested in being the lead investor and managing the hotel if I could get some additional backing. So, I took them around town . . . We talked to bankers and met everybody. About this time, I called Herbert McAdams, and he suggested I go to the EDA [Economic Development Administration] and see if we couldn't get a loan for a basis to start this thing. So I did. This was about late summer, '78 or '79. We called on the EDA and ended up making an application through the office in Dallas. As it turns out it was the end of their fiscal year, and they actually had some extra money in their budget! Imagine that! They explained that if we could get the application in by September 1 that they would certainly give it serious consideration. I didn't know what to do then. I wasn't a hotel guy and didn't write grant or loan applications. I'm no financier. That's when another "coincidence" happened.

I was over at the Capital one day. We had the front doors open, and we had some workers inside. Then from nowhere this nice-looking guy walks into the lobby and said "Are you connected to this thing?" I said, "Yes, I am." And he said, "My name is Charles Bland and I build hotels. This is my business!"

Then Bland tells me what a gem of a place the Capital could be. It took someone like Bland who had been in the business to see the vision. So anyway he says he wishes he could be a part of it and I say, "Son, you've got a part of it. You're in!" Bland didn't know what he got into.

There was another guy by the name of Lawrence Walters, who had gone to hotel school. He was from Little Rock. Lawrence Walters had a contact through some bond people here that told him what I was trying to do. So he called me and said that he wanted to know more about it. His family had just sold something, and they had some money.

Walters's family had come from Malvern, and at that time they were well-to-do and had some money. He said that he would like to get into this thing. All of a sudden the three of us got together and formed the Capital Hotel Partnership, something entirely different than what I spent two years doing. We just threw the other stuff out and started over again. All of a sudden we had all this pressure on us to get this application in to the EDA. Charles Bland sat down and just worked overnight and wrote the application. Only a hotel man could have done it. We could not have done it without Charles Bland. He put this application together and had to get a few testimonials around town about how it was needed and how many people would be employed.

The loan got approved for $1,750,000.00. We thought that was on-ice. Suddenly, we got a notice from the EDA that said they could not allow this loan. This happened during the transition in the White House between Carter and Reagan. Some bureaucrat in Washington decided to pull the rug out from under us. Meanwhile, we had gotten a commitment from the Metro Center committee: they had approved us for a $4.25 million bond issue. So we had financing and that was something that no one could get anywhere; that put us in really good shape. We had a Metro Center tax-free improvement bond. Then this bureaucrat from Washington writes us and says they could not make the loan because now the other part of the project is financed with tax-free bonds. So we pick up the phone and call David Pryor. We hop on a plane and flew to Washington. David just dropped everything on his agenda, left his office. We just hotfooted it around Washington. Thanks to Pryor we got the EDA loan straightened out.

So we thought we lost out, but we were back in the saddle again. This was all happening while we were talking to the Lincoln Hotels people; Joe McCarthy was president then. So we went back and got on the thing again. By the time we had all of this worked out, Lincoln had decided that they had a lot of people and they wanted to go to work and do something, so they said if you can make the financing work, why, we'll take it on. So they went to New York and raised the equity, a little over three million dollars. They put some money in, and we put some money in, and off we went. But it was amazing how things fit together, and the timing was perfect in that respect. It could never happen again, and it was amazing that it happened then.

It had such community support. I had never been connected to a project that had as much community support as that one did

The Final Deal

Senator Pryor and Watt Gregory, from the Rose firm, were key in helping Cromwell reverse the denial of the EDA grant that had initially been approved. Eventually a $9 million package was put together. The *Arkansas Gazette* summarized the finance and deal-making proceedings as follows:

> Two experienced hotel men—Charles Bland and Lawrence Walters— came to Cromwell and said they were looking for a hotel. The three men formed a partnership and went looking for money.
>
> At this point the public sector made some important contributions to the project: The Metrocenter Improvement District Commission approved

Joe McCarthy *(left)*, president of the Lincoln Hotel Group, and Ed Cromwell. Lincoln Hotels, an offshoot of a large nationwide development firm, had recently started developing hotels and was specializing in renovating old ones such as the Capital. (Arkansas Democrat-Gazette)

a $4.25 million tax exempt bond issue to help finance the project. The Economic Development Administration agreed to make a low-interest loan of $1.75 million. The state Historic Preservation Program obtained a $164,000 grant to pay for research and planning.

Then the partnership went searching for someone to manage the property and to provide more capital. They found Lincoln Hotels, an offshoot of a large nationwide development firm. The company had recently started developing hotels and was specializing in renovating old ones. "Because of high interest rates they were at a slowdown in their development," Cromwell said. "And here we were with a financial package all ready. Today they wouldn't be interested in a 123-room hotel in a town the size of Little Rock."

It would be impossible to put together the same financial package today, Cromwell said, because the tax laws governing such projects have been changed. He credited U.S. Senator David Pryor with keeping the Capital project eligible when those changes were being made.

Another thing that interested Lincoln officials about the Capital was the Excelsior Hotel and convention center being built across the street. The absence of such a compatible development was "one problem we had with the original partnership," [Cromwell] said.

Lincoln is now the primary owner of the Capital, but Cromwell, Bland and Walters kept a small financial interest in the hotel.

(*Arkansas Gazette,* December 19, 1983)

In 1980 the deal was finally put together and the stage was set for restoration of the Capital Hotel.

The Miracle On Markham Street, Part Two

The Beginning of Restoration

In 1980, with money in-hand, Cromwell hired and paid Ned Shank, the historic preservationist, to conduct research on the Capital Hotel. Ned and his wife, the writer and poet Crescent Dragonwagon, were also innkeepers, having owned and operated one of the first bed-and-breakfast establishments in Eureka Springs: The Inn at Dairy Hollow. Ned would spend several months meticulously digging through newspaper archives, city directories, and the musty files of the historic preservation offices in town. His research was compiled for Cromwell and submitted in several draft forms: "The Capital Hotel: A Historical Narrative of Its Early History, Uses and Appearance."

While Ned Shank was completing his historical research, Cromwell's firm (Cromwell, Neyland, Truemper, Levy and Gatchell) worked with the CPA firm, Laventhol and Horwath to write a comprehensive business plan for the "Proposed restoration and expansion of the Capital Hotel." The plan was approved, and work began in earnest on the restoration of the Capital which was boarded-up and vacant.

Structural Restoration

The two point men on the restoration of the hotel were Guner Eruren, project structural engineer, and Jim Pfeifer, project architect. An initial survey of the building showed that the hundred-year-old wood beams were almost as strong as steel, although many of the floors were sagging. The original plaster walls provided immense soundproofing and absorption of noise and vibration.

Scott Martin, a bearded, twenty-nine-year-old, six-one, two-hundred-plus pounder with experience in home building and construction reported to Guner Eruren and was the field engineer on the project.

> When I first went in, the place had been boarded up since it had last been used. The worst part of it was the people that frequented the place. When we would come in the morning, you know you would have to be careful and look around the place . . . Sometimes people would be running out. When we would walk up to the fourth floor, you could hear people running out of the place. One day, we went in and there was a guy sweeping floors. We didn't think anything of him . . . just thought he was part of our clean-up crew. But as soon as we walked past, we heard the broom hit the floor, and the guy was running out the door. It was pretty funny. We couldn't keep people out. They would play funny little games in the room at night. There would be candles and strange magazines and strange things went on there at night. There were all sorts of transients. They would get off there at the bus station next door and go right to the Capital where they would come in through the basement.

Left: Another interior view of the Capital Hotel lobby looking from the back toward the front of the hotel on the second-floor mezzanine level. (Arkansas Democrat-Gazette)

Right: Interior shot of the Capital Hotel lobby during the first phase of the restoration. Paint chips were taken from the walls and studied in order to determine the original paint colors used in the hotel. (Arkansas Democrat-Gazette)

Above: Restoration begins: Howell and Jackson were the general contractors who supervised the entire project including refurbishing of the cast-iron façade. *(Cromwell Architects and Engineers, Inc.)*

Below: Work begins on the Excelsior Hotel and State House Convention Center across the street from the Capital. *(Cromwell Architects and Engineers, Inc.)*

Above left: Scott Martin, field engineer. *(Cromwell Architects and Engineers, Inc.)*

Above right: Guner Eruren, project structural engineer. *(Cromwell Architects and Engineers, Inc.)*

Left: Jim Pfeifer, *left,* project architect and one of the contractors from Howell and Jackson. Pfeifer supervised the project once the structural changes had been made to the building. Pfeifer acquired and used a collection of old postcards to give him clues regarding the design of the original building, including the lettering on the front of the hotel. *(Cromwell Architects and Engineers, Inc.)*

While the building was basically sound, many of the floors sagged because of the ill-supported load incurred when the fourth floor was built in 1890. Cromwell and Eruren decided that a steel structure had to be built within the existing building: a building within a building. This new steel structure would support the outside walls. The existing floors had been weakened when modern plumbing had been installed; workers had simply cut through the floor joists.

Cromwell and his crew discovered that the original 1872 Denckla building had been constructed from used lumber. Scott Martin said, "When we were underneath the ground floor and taking pictures of it, we discovered the lumber had been used. It was full of nails on the other side. They had taken used lumber and turned the planks over and used the good side."

During the clean out of the hotel structure, workmen discovered lots of different condom tins and bottles; there was quite a little collection of light bulbs and electrical gear that showed the history of the light bulb. Martin recalls: "We even found a hidden bathroom that had been used when it was a European-style hotel at the turn of the century when they had just one bathroom on every floor." Eventually the artifacts were turned over and put on display at the Old State House.

Richard Allin, editor at the *Gazette* actually wrote a column asking for the return of artifacts that might be in the possession of former guests. "Bits and pieces of hotel items went astray during the hotel's decline . . ." (*Arkansas Gazette,* December 23,

Opposite and above: The Capital Hotel in the '70s prior to Ed Cromwell's restoration efforts, was in severe decay. There was a billiard hall on the ground floor of the hotel that catered to unsavory transients who arrived at the adjacent bus station. The Capital Hotel and its immediate environs was a mecca for bums, thieves, and prostitutes. When Cromwell's original investor group bought the hotel property from Elizabeth Cassinelli, the Capital was boarded up in an attempt to keep out trespassers. *(Cromwell Architects and Engineers, Inc.)*

Above left: Detail of the deterioration of the cast-iron façade of the Capital Hotel prior to restoration begun in 1980. Herman Bemberg, who founded Bemberg Iron Works, came out of retirement to personally supervise the restoration work on the façade. *(Cromwell Architects and Engineers, Inc.)*

Above right: The lobby at the start of restoration. Note that the glass skylight had already been removed for safe-keeping and refurbishing. *(Cromwell Architects and Engineers, Inc.)*

Right: Front view of the Capital Hotel just prior to restoration. The building was in such a state of deterioration that, as Jim Pfeifer, project architect, recalls, there was a lot of skepticism about how the Capital might ever be restored to Ed Cromwell's vision and design. *(Cromwell Architects and Engineers, Inc.)*

Guner Eruren, project structural engineer, conducted the
initial survey of the Capital
that showed the building's one-
hundred-year-old stone foundation seen here and its wood
beams were in good condition,
although many of the upper
hotel floors were sagging.
*(Cromwell Architects and
Engineers, Inc.)*

Right: Another interior photograph of the Capital Hotel lobby looking from the back toward the front of the hotel on the second-floor mezzanine level. (Arkansas Democrat-Gazette)

Opposite top: During the clean-out phase of the restoration, workers found a variety of old artifacts from antique light bulbs and condom tins to old wallpaper and hotel china. These items were put on display at an exhibit at the Old State House Museum and included a hotel guest book from 1927 and 1928 and a recast capital shown here. (Arkansas Democrat-Gazette)

Opposite bottom: Capital Hotel guest book pages from 1927 to 1928. During this period, the Capital Hotel was a place for parties and society events including the wedding reception Ed Cromwell attended when he first came to Little Rock in 1935. (Arkansas Democrat-Gazette)

1983). Among the items that were displayed at the Old State House were "wallpaper samples, etched-glass transoms, photographs, a silver sugar bowl, china, and a desk register."

Martin remembers Ed Cromwell being at the worksite: "Every day from start to finish, just wandering around, loving it. It was his dream home and once it got started, he was there every day. Not actively involved in it, just there."

Kent Taylor, another Cromwell staffer who would work on a series of Stephens, Inc.–related projects, including the restoration of the Stephens' Five Main Place Building, remembers wandering through the Capital Hotel on his lunch break:

> I went there on break-time, morning, afternoon and lunchtime. I found some real interesting things such as a piece of the plasterwork in the dining room—some of it is exposed in the kitchen right now. I have a collection of wallpaper that came from high up in the building when it was in its late

THE CAPITAL HOTEL

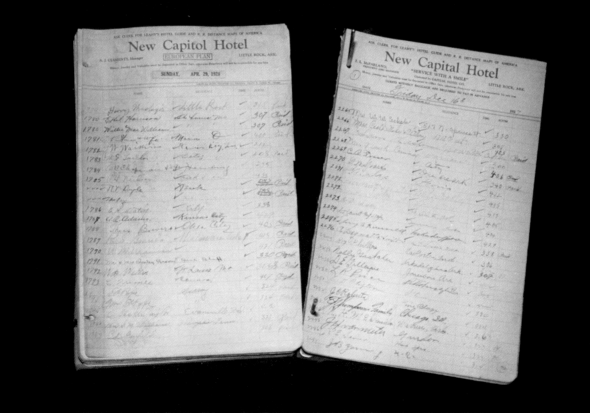

When Cromwell and his original investor group bought the Capital Hotel from Elizabeth Cassinelli, they had the stained-glass skylight seen in this photograph, removed for cleaning and for safe-keeping during the restoration process. (*Cromwell Architects and Engineers, Inc.*)

Victorian heyday. It was gold and red, just real gaudy. Interestingly, two layers of wallpaper came from underneath the marble in the lobby adjacent to the passenger elevator. They had just taken the marble off and were astonished to find two layers of wallpaper under the marble, and I figured that it came from when it was an office building before it became a hotel.

Old Postcards and New Information

In addition to the physical surveys, and the research conducted by Ned Shank, the restoration team used a variety of resources to recreate what the Capital Hotel was like when it first opened. Jim Pfeifer, the project engineer, recalls studying old postcards printed around 1908:

> We used those postcards for actual restoration purpose. These were some really good documents that showed the color types of awnings. We didn't always follow things exactly. The Lincoln Hotel people had their input and the Historic Preservation people wanted a mix of colors: they didn't want a red and green hotel. Some things—such as the old cartouche on top of the building and long since gone—we decided not to restore or replace. One of the cards shows the lettering up here of the Capital Hotel and we recreated the lettering up there.

7449. New Capitol Hotel, Little Rock, Ark.

Little Rock, Ark.   2371   west Markham Street

I. Goodman, Publisher, Little Rock, Ark.

Markham Street, west from Main,

Little Rock, Ark.

Old Postcards Give New Information

In addition to the physical surveys and the research conducted by Ned Shank, the restoration team used a variety of resources to re-create what the Capital Hotel was like when it first opened. Jim Pfeifer, the project engineer, recalls studying old postcards printed around 1908: "We used those postcards for actual restoration purpose. These were some really good documents that showed the color types of awnings. We didn't always follow things exactly. The Lincoln Hotel people had their input and the Historic Preservation people wanted a mix of colors; they didn't want a red and green hotel. Some things, such as the old cartouche on top of the building, and long since gone, we decided not to restore or replace. One of the cards shows the lettering up here of the Capital Hotel, and we recreated that lettering."

Many of these postcards were printed and hand colored in Germany. The collection of cards is provided courtesy of Jim Pfeifer from his personal collection.

Top: New Capital Hotel after final fourth floor addition in 1908.

Middle: View of West Markham Street with Capital Hotel to the immediate right.

Bottom: Another view of West Markham from the opposite direction. The Capital Hotel is the second building on the left.

Top: This postcard shows the Capital Hotel rotunda after the remodeling design by George Mann. A significant figure in Arkansas's architectural heritage, Mann's work included the State Capitol, Arkansas Gazette and Donaghey Buildings, the Pulaski County Courthouse, and the Marion Hotel. His 1908 alterations to the Capital Hotel storefronts, and rotunda provided the hotel with a modernizing facelift and opened up the lobby space into a more unified and impressive area.

Middle: Original lobby designed by George Mann, the architect who also did the last alterations to the Capital Hotel in 1908.

Bottom: Another view of West Markham with the Capital Hotel on the left.

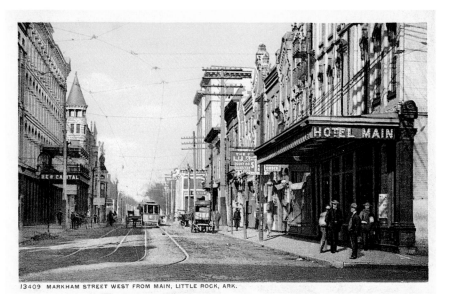

NEW CAPITAL HOTEL, LITTLE ROCK, ARK.

7747. Capital Hotel, Little Rock, Ark.

Top: The New Capital Hotel.

Bottom: The Capital Hotel after 1908, showing such details as the design band color of the hotel canopies.

The Realization of the Vision

As the restoration continued, there was an intensified interest in the project by the general public and news media. "We didn't need an ad agency or public relations firm on this hotel," recalled Pfeifer. "All you had to do was call the local newspaper and tell them what was going on—next thing you know we'd have a front page story."

To illustrate his point, Pfeifer remembers that he went to work one day to find a backhoe digging a hole next to the Capital in preparation for installing a gigantic traffic light signal box and light pole fixture. "We went over and couldn't get anywhere with the city . . . so we called over to the newspaper and said, 'Look they're getting ready to shine a light in General Grant's room!'" On January 29, 1983, the

Work begins in earnest on the Capital Hotel. Here a worker sandblasts the façade on the front of Capital Hotel. (Arkansas Democrat-Gazette)

Gazette ran a front page story: "Architects Upset over Plans to Install Signal Next to Hotel." "We had a huge amount of public support," said Pfeifer. " It was like the whole state owned this hotel and was working on it. It was pretty wild." Needless to say, the city made alternative arrangements in placing the signal box.

To motivate workers and to communicate the vision, Pfeifer had one of the artist's colored drawings of a restored Capital blown up into poster size and placed in the lobby of the hotel. "The workmen just dropped their jaws and said there was no way that the lobby was going to look like that. But it inspired them. Somehow there was a 'magic' on that construction site. It cost a lot of money, and some of the people that were pumping it in didn't necessarily always think there was magic. There were a lot of issues that came up that were hard to deal with. Overall, it was something that I had never seen before. I saw some of the most hard-ass contractors that I've ever known around here that were encouraging others to work together and get the job done and not argue about small things. It was quite a process."

As the restoration continued, there was an intensified interest and support of the restoration project by the general public and the news media. For example, when the City of Little Rock started digging an immense hole to install a gigantic traffic-light signal box and light-pole fixture, the *Gazette* ran a front-page article along with this photograph. The article headline read, "Architects Upset Over Plans to Install Signal Next to Hotel." Only days after the article appeared and the city received a flood of phone calls, alternative arrangements were made in placing the signal box and light pole. (Arkansas Democrat-Gazette)

Continued Restoration

Once Guner Eruren had completed the structural part of the job, he turned the project over to Jim Pfeifer. "A lot of the rest of it just followed your ordinary building construction timetable," said Pfeifer. "You put in your systems: your electrical and mechanical, and then your finishes. In the lobby area, we climbed up scaffolding and took paint chips all the way down from every item from base to decoration. They were all painted some pink. It was all a pinky-beige. We put them under a microscope and found that this was a bronzing compound. The tile on the lobby floor was in bad condition. Winburn Tile was the local manufacturing company. They actually matched tile where we had heaving. The tile workmen matched the pattern."

Almost Forgotten Skills

Jim Pfeifer said, "A lot of this plaster was down, we had to cast it. Howell and Jackson, the contractors, brought some guys out of retirement. Old pros. They actually set up a plaster shop in the back of the hotel. They'd take off the ornate grapes at the tops of the columns and put them in sand and make an imprint. Then they would pour rubber liquid and make a cast or form. Then they would pour plaster in there, and it would come out looking like the original, and they would stick it up there."

R. J. Van Portfliet and his partner Odell Carpenter were the "old pros" Pfeifer referred to. On June 27, 1983, the *Gazette* reported,

> . . . when the hotel was built in 1877, it took a crew of 30 plasterers to complete the work. In the century since, some of the plaster has been broken. More of it was destroyed by water leaking in from the skylight . . . It [restoring the plaster] is touchy work that will require an estimated 5,000 pounds of molding plaster . . . Some pieces, such as the clusters of fruit crowning the columns, can be cast in a small shop set up just off the lobby, then affixed whole sections at a time. Other repairs call for running the plaster in place; that is shaping it while still wet on the wall by means of a metal template. Corners are done freehand. "Some of these patterns could have originated in the days of the pyramids," Van Portfliet said. "The trade's been around that long, and the patterns have sort of been passed on through the years . . . There aren't too many of us doing this kind of work anymore . . . my partner and I are out of Hot Springs. They brought us out of retirement to do the job. I've got to be honest—it's a dying trade."

In addition to the plastering work, there were other reconstruction hurdles. Pfeifer recounts:

> Of course the outside of the building was a challenge, too. It was cast iron up to the third floor. The front of the fourth story was wood with sheet metal around it. It had some iron rusted off, and we had to call Herman Bemberg of Bemberg Iron Works. He took samples from the top of the columns that were rusted off and recast them. People loved working on the project. Bemberg built all the I-beams and bridges and stuff. Mr. Bemberg was getting on in years, but he was tremendously excited about working on the Capital. He would personally come out there with a guy, and they would

unscrew some of the cast-iron façade and take it back to their shop and experiment to find out what kind of metal would be best to use.

We didn't want to disturb the plaster on the second floor of the lobby, so we tore up the floor instead and ran the ducts and all the wiring in the floor of the second floor to avoid that.

There were a lot of trade-offs in this building: adding modern conveniences, yet keeping as much of the original building intact as possible. For example, we built completely new fire stairs that went all the way to the top down to the exit on the street and fully sprinkled the building. It was like a treasure hunt to see how the workers could run these pipes to be as little exposed as possible.

A series of articles appeared in the *Democrat* and *Gazette* at the time the renovation was being finished. The first article begins by quoting Jim Pfeifer and detailing the renovation plan: "Capital Reopening 'Miracle' Of Markham Street, 'Demanded' By Little Rock":

The Howell and Jackson Construction Company of North Little Rock was hired as the main contractor, and several subcontracts were issued for specialized work. Construction started early this year.

"They went through here like a tornado," Pfeifer said. "I've seen jobs like this take two years." Rick Brown was in charge of the large construction crew, which had to deal not only with heavy jobs such as pouring new concrete

This page and opposite: Two "old pros," retired plasterers, R. J. Van Portfliet and his partner Odell Carpenter, came out of retirement to help in the restoration. Much of the work, as seen in these photographs was done freehand. (Arkansas Democrat-Gazette)

floors and putting in steel reinforcements, but also had to do detail work such as bronzing the capitals on the columns and replacing stained glass.

A sprinkler system was hidden throughout the building, a modern fire alarm system installed, buckled tiles were matched and replaced, the original globe lights were reinstalled, wood molding details were reproduced and used throughout the hotel. An elevator large enough to hold a luncheon meeting was installed.

Some areas, such as the lobby and mezzanine, were faithfully restored to George R. Mann's 1908 design. Wilson Stiles of the state Historic Preservation Program took paint samples and studied them under a microscope to determine what colors should be used. Turn-of-the-century carbon filament bulbs were reproduced to give a golden glow around the lobby's stained glass skylight. Cromwell managed to save almost all of the original stained glass in the building.

Some of Mann's designs were altered slightly to meet present day codes. For instance, the bronze railings around the second floor of the atrium were raised four inches to keep people from falling over them into the lobby.

Outside of the lobby, some things were altered considerably. The restaurant and bar are designed to complement Mann's lobby, but they aren't reproductions of former establishments. Some original details were kept in the guest rooms, such as the window frames and high ceilings. But mostly they are brand new rooms with all the modern conveniences that travelers expect.

And, there is the addition to the south end of the building. The rooms look the same as the ones in the older part of the building, but in these, even the window frames are new.

On the outside, a parking lot was constructed underneath the three-story rear addition. There will be valet parking. However, there are fewer parking spaces than there are rooms. The hotel expects that many of its guests to arrive by plane.

Everyone knew the restoration of the original cast-iron front would be impressive. But Stiles said he and others have been "really excited" concerning the west façade pop out. No one realized it would be that attractive when it was cleaned up, he said.

Pfeifer said that originally it was thought some of the detailed, artistic work would have to be imported from outside the state. But all of the talent was found locally, he said, and "they bent over backwards to give us superior work."

R. J. Van Portfliet did the ornamental plaster work. Jim Pozza replaced missing or damaged marble. Herman Bemberg recast some of the iron façade. Nick Howell, Rick Brown and O. C. Strayhorn of Howell and Jackson ran the carpentry crew that did the detailed woodwork. Andy Zawacki, a woodcarver, repaired the old ballroom mantle. Jerry Hoffman and Jimmy Smith of J. E. Beard Paint Company rebronzed all of the decorative plaster in the lobby. Charles Carpenter of Architectural Antiques refinished and restored the original light fixtures.

(*Arkansas Gazette,* December 19, 1983)

One of the craftsmen not mentioned by name in the above text, according to Bill Worthen, is Joel Railsback, manager for Mashburn Stained Glass, who restored the stained glass, including the lobby skylight.

A second article, published two months prior to the hotel's reopening, gives us additional insights and information about the restoration as well as the sense of pride felt by everyone involved with the project:

Capital Renovation Nearing Completion
BY JEFF THATCHER
DEMOCRAT STAFF WRITER

Amidst the dust, the debris, the hammering and the continuous chatter of workmen, a modern-day phoenix is rising from the rubble in downtown Little Rock. Known as the Capital Hotel, this fine-feathered landmark is rapidly approaching its original splendor.

"We are on schedule," said Jim Pfeifer, the harried-looking project architect from the Little Rock firm of Cromwell, Truemper, Levy, Parker & Woodsmall Inc. "It will be open in December.

The Capital Hotel was in such a state of disrepair that it was hard for anyone to imagine that the building could be adequately restored. To motivate workers and to communicate the vision, Ed Cromwell and Jim Pfeifer commissioned an artist to do several colored drawings of a restored Capital Hotel. These drawings were blown up to poster size and placed in the lobby of the hotel to inspire workers. (*Cromwell Architects and Engineers, Inc.*)

While the building was basically sound, many of the floors sagged because of the ill-supported load of the fourth floor added in 1890. Ed Cromwell and Guner Eruren decided that a steel structure had to be built within the existing building: a building within a building. This new steel structure would be built to support the outside walls. *(Cromwell Architects and Engineers, Inc.)*

"It has been a stupendous task," Pfeifer said, "but the project has made the workmen proud of what they are doing."

Major structural changes were implemented in the Capital renovation, Pfeifer said, "Predominantly, the building has been made structurally sound and fireproofed in terms of a safety system. The lobby is also being restored very accurately with the help of the state preservation society. The finishes are being done stringently to accommodate the Lincoln Hotels' standard of quality."

As he moved enthusiastically through the Capital while conducting a tour, Pfeifer pointed out some of the aspects of the building that will be most notable. "Here is an enormous passenger elevator that is at least 10 feet by 15 feet in diameter," he said. "It may be the largest passenger elevator in the country. Over there, the front desk will be marble with the old teller cages intact. The old safe door has even been retained. But computers have replaced the old vaults. The dining room will be off to the left of the lobby and will be furnished elegantly."

With 123 rooms and 100,000 square feet of space, Pfeifer confessed that the Capital has been a voluminous undertaking. "The cooperation has been tremendous, however," he said. "We have used all local labor and all local

Left: An intricate scaffolding in the lobby allowed workers to access the skylight. *(Cromwell Architects and Engineers, Inc.)*

Right: Upper-floor interior during restoration. A layer of specially formulated, light concrete was poured to level the floors. *(Cromwell Architects and Engineers, Inc.)*

contractors. One of the plasterers has been nominated for 'craftsman of the year' for his work on the project." Moving from room to room like a child showing off a favorite toy, Pfeifer continually pointed out unique and innovative efforts on the part of the workers.

"Our engineers have been spectacular in their work," he said. "They installed a complete sprinkler and fire alarm system that is the most sophisticated one available. A lightweight concrete slurry was also poured over the floor to soundproof the rooms. The ceramic is patterned after the lobby floors and the wallpaper is representative of an artist's work. There are just a lot of small things that we are proud of."

"Everyone feels that they almost own a part of the hotel," he said. "There's a lot of pride in the project. There has just been a tremendous groundswell of support."

The color scheme will include bronzing of an ornamental design and light gold on many of the paint surfaces "derived from scrapings that we made from the original paint," Pfeifer said.

(*Arkansas Democrat,* October 9, 1983)

Top: Exposed arch showing original brick and wood construction. *(Cromwell Architects and Engineers, Inc.)*

Bottom: As part of the structural reconfiguring, columns were cut in two, and reinforced structural steel members added before the columns were restored. *(Cromwell Architects and Engineers, Inc.)*

Top: Damage to the lobby floor was extensive because of water seeping down in cracks and then freezing. Winburn Tile Company replicated the original tile and did the restoration of the lobby floor. *(Cromwell Architects and Engineers, Inc.)*

Bottom: Detail of dentil work and a Corinthian column that were recast. *(Cromwell Architects and Engineers, Inc.)*

Top: This wall tie is a structural member used to tie the masonry to the structure of the building. *(Cromwell Architects and Engineers, Inc.)*

Bottom: Workers took pains to record and save as many decorative items as possible. Sample of old wallpaper behind the hotel vault shows some of the original stenciling. *(Cromwell Architects and Engineers, Inc.)*

When the restoration began, these columns were painted pink. Workers stripped all the paint away and found that all the columns in the lobby were scagliola. In 1908, it was considered fashionable to simulate marble materials instead of having the real thing. *(Cromwell Architects and Engineers, Inc.)*

Another unusual project was the marbling of the columns, which was actually completed several weeks after the hotel reopened for business. "Malcolm Robson . . . a fifth generation marbler and grainer and his assistant, Joni Monnich, spent the week marbleizing 42 plaster columns in the lobby and mezzanine of the Capital . . . A native of London, England . . . Robson commissions have included Buckingham Palace, the House of Parliament and the Athenaeum in Philadelphia" (*Arkansas Democrat,* January 19, 1984).

Yet another article gives us details of the decorative painting process known as scagliola: a method of reproducing the marbled effect on the hotel columns:

Painting of Lobby Columns
One of Few Touches Left

A person walking into the Capital Hotel lobby today will see basically the finished product. However, there are a few touches yet to be applied. One of them is the painting of the lobby's ornate columns to make them look like marble.

The columns, built during a 1908 renovation, were made of plaster, and they were given a marble appearance by a process called scagliola. In that process, plaster is mixed with finely ground gypsum, marble dust and glue and the columns are covered with the mixture. When it dries, the exteriors of the columns are rock hard and look like marble.

"This is all man-made. There is nothing real about this at all," said Wilson Stiles of the Historic Preservation Program of the state Natural and Cultural Heritage Department as he knocked his knuckles against one of the columns during a recent tour of the building.

The original 42 columns cracked and had to be repaired with plaster. Instead of using the scagliola process on them again, this time they will be painted to look like marble.

That job has been given to Malcolm Robson, who has painted columns at Buckingham Palace, Windsor Palace and Mount Vernon. He will arrive January 16 to start painting the columns. He will give a lecture and demonstration on his work at 5 P.M. January 19 at the hotel. The demonstration is sponsored by Lincoln Hotels, the principal owner of the hotel, and the Historic Preservation Program.

Stiles said a portion of one of the columns would keep part of its scagliola exterior so people can compare it with the painting technique.

(*Arkansas Gazette,* December 19, 1983)

Among Ed Cromwell's files is a list of all the subcontractors who worked on the project:

General Contractor	Howell & Jackson Construction Co.
Cast-iron Architecture restoration	Bemberg Iron
Stained Glass restoration	Mashburn Stained Glass
Light fixture restoration	Architectural Antiques
Electrical	Bradshaw Electric
Mechanical & Plumbing	Arkansas Mechanical Contractors

The old passenger elevator, here, was replaced at Ed Cromwell's insistence with the largest elevator that Otis made at the time, which is similar design and size to those used at the World Trade Center towers. *(Cromwell Architects and Engineers, Inc.)*

Sprinkler System	Masco, Inc.
Grilles	AirTech
Steel	Jacksonville Steel
Sheet Metal	Custom Sheet Metal
Tile Mfg.	Winburn Tile
Glazing	PPG
Millwork	Advance Mfg. Company
Paint	J. E. Beard Painting
Plaster and Drywall	Kirk Plastering Company
Roofing	Ketcher & Company
Hardware	P. C. Hardware
Fire Alarm	Triple-S Alarm Co.
Lighting Consultant	Candace Kling
Kitchen Consultant	Gene Rise

And so with a cast of hundreds and after almost two decades, the Capital Hotel opened for business on December 19, 1983.

Lincoln Hotels had selected Charles Stoermer to be the general manager. In an interview five years after the opening of the hotel, Stoermer told about his life and career in the hotel industry.

Humble Start Leads Manager
to Luxury of Capital Hotel
BY HOWARD COAN
DEMOCRAT BUSINESS WRITER

Charles Stoermer, General Manager of the Capital Hotel in Little Rock, admits he came from humble beginnings growing up in the war-torn German city of Hamburg. He didn't even start school until World War II ended in 1945 and he was already eight years old. His formal education stopped seven years later. Despite that, he feels "very lucky" because his family's one-bedroom apartment somehow survived the heavy bombing of Hamburg, while "everything around us was gone."

"I remember in 1944 and 1945 my mother and I moved out of the city into the country because of the bombing," he said in an interview last week.

British forces had captured his father, a German Army draftee given the task of stringing up telephone lines in Norway. He remained a prisoner until the war's end. The months immediately after the war were possibly the worst time. Food was scarce and his family often went hungry.

"We couldn't find anything to eat, so they often went into the country-side to beg for food." At 15, he entered a three-year hotel apprenticeship. Every day he wore his one white shirt which his mother washed daily. "I couldn't play soccer because I only had one pair of shoes."

Three years later, Stoermer decided to leave West Germany for the United States, even though he spoke almost no English. He lived with an aunt in Queens in New York for the first six months. He also studied English on his own while working as a waiter "I learned the language by spending hours and hours in movie houses," he said.

His 27-year career with Hilton Hotels eventually led to work at the

Above: In order to make the hotel economically viable, a new three-story addition was built on the south end of the building. The rooms in the new addition were carefully constructed to blend in with the rest of the hotel. Underneath the addition is room for valet parking. *(Cromwell Architects and Engineers, Inc.)*

Right: As noted in the signage that was displayed outside the hotel, the restoration project was completed by Howell and Jackson contractors. Funding was provided by the Metrocenter Improvement District Commission which approved a $4.25 million tax-exempt bond issue. The Economic Development Administration also agreed to make a low-interest loan of $1.75 million. The State Historic Preservation Program obtained a $164,000 grant to pay for research and planning. *(Cromwell Architects and Engineers, Inc.)*

CAPITAL HOTEL

a tradition in hospitality · est. 1877

MANAGING PARTNER AND OPERATOR:

LINCOLN HOTELS

CONTRACTOR:
HOWELL & JACKSON

ARCHITECT:
CROMWELL, TRUEMPER, LEVY, PARKER & WOODSMALL

INTERIORS:
ABV & ASSOCIATES

THE RESTORATION OF THE CAPITAL HOTEL WHICH IS LISTED ON THE NATIONAL REGISTER OF HISTORIC PLACES, HAS BEEN FUNDED WITH THE ASSISTANCE OF A MATCHING GRANT-IN-AID FROM THE ARKANSAS HISTORIC PRESERVATION PROGRAM AND THE DEPARTMENT OF INTERIOR, NATIONAL PARK SERVICE, UNDER PROVISION OF THE NATIONAL HISTORIC PRESERVATION ACT OF 1966 AS AMENDED

Plaza and Waldorf Astoria in New York, and the Palmer House in Chicago, among others.

In those early years, "I earned a lot of money as a waiter by working 16–18 hours day. I made $400–$500 a week at that time."

He moved up to dining room captain at the Plaza Hotel and maitre d'hotel at the Peacock Alley and Marco Polo Club at the Waldorf Astoria. "I enjoyed being a maitre d'. That part of my career was fun and glamorous. Every day was exciting."

He later spent 10 years handling the food and beverage operation at the 1,100-room Washington Hilton. He left that hotel for short time to go to the Atlanta Hilton and to help in the reopening of the Fairmont Hotel in Philadelphia.

Five years after leaving West Germany, Stoermer became a U.S. citizen. He also served in the U.S. Army from 1962–64. He attended the Army's cooking school, then worked as a cook at an officers' club in Fort Monroe, Va. "It was a very good experience."

When he came to Little Rock in June 1983 the Capital Hotel had been out of business for six years. The hotel appeared ready for the wrecker's ball

The railing seen here is the original brass rail surrounding the mezzanine atrium. For safety purposes additional ironwork was added and the rail raised. *(Cromwell Architects and Engineers, Inc.)*

during his first inspection trip. "It was totally boarded up. The floors were broken. The plaster was coming down from the ceiling. It was a wreck."

But Stoermer, 51, visualized what the hotel could be. Now when the stocky, 6-foot-3 Stoermer sits in his small, narrow office on the Capital's mezzanine, framed photos of some famous guests at his hotel stare back at him, including Sen. and Mrs. Dan Quayle, Sen. Robert Dole, Michael Dukakis, Jimmy Carter and Henry Kissinger. He has a thank-you note from Vice President George Bush after a 1984 visit, saying "It's a great place to stay."

Stoermer knew about hotel renovation. He was director of food and beverage operations at the Fairmont Hotel when it reopened. The new hotel replaced the Bellevue Stratford, which had closed down after several guests died of Legionnaires' Disease.

The Capital's year-long renovation cost $10 million including $4.5 million in tax-free Metrocentre Improvement District revenue bonds. Stoermer was involved in the last six months of the renovation.

"I still marvel at the people who worked on this hotel—the carpenters, plumbers. Even after five years it's holding up. The workmanship was just incredible."

The 123-room hotel at Markham and Louisiana streets reopened in December 1983. The building, which is listed on the National Register of Historic Places, was built as an office building in 1872 and converted into a hotel in 1877.

By the early part of the 20th century, the hotel had become a center of political and social life in the state. The revived hotel has also turned into a success. Stoermer said the hotel is performing "better and better" from year to year. He attributes this in large part to business generated by the hotel catering service and Ashley's restaurant.

"Because of the restaurant and catering, this hotel is extremely successful."

In 1987, the hotel ranked 55th among center-city hotels in a national survey by Lodging Hospitality magazine. Each room in the Capital produced about $36,000 in annual revenue and total sales exceeded $4.4 million.

This year, occupancy is 1,500 rooms above last year, and the occupancy rate has climbed 5 percent. The average room rate is also a little higher. Other reasons for the improved business include more repeat customers and an increasing number of conventions in Little Rock.

Room rates have remained at a moderate level for a luxury hotel, compared to some larger cities. The Capital, Stoermer points out, features a $77 a night corporate rate and a $69 weekend special, along with a two-bedroom suite priced at $285 a night.

On weeknights, the tourist rate ranges from $79 to $99 a night depending on room size and location.

With these rates, Stoermer avoids discouraging those people who want to splurge for a night or two without breaking their budgets. "If the hotel was standing somewhere on Fifth Avenue in New York, I wouldn't survive as a manager doing this. My owners would kick me out. But we're still an excellent product that you can afford."

At this point, Stoermer runs the hotel independently. "There was talk of putting a hotel management company in here, but they decided to let me handle it by myself."

Opposite: Interior view of the skylight and lobby atrium after completion of the restoration. (Arkansas Democrat-Gazette)

Top: Outside view of the Capital Hotel as it looked on December 19, 1983, the day it reopened for business. (Arkansas Democrat-Gazette)

Bottom: The marbleized columns in the lobby and the mezzanine of the Capital Hotel were constructed as part of George Mann's 1908 renovation. The columns were made of plaster, and they were given a marble appearance by a process called scagliola. In that process, plaster is mixed with finely ground gypsum, marble dust, and glue and the columns are covered with the mixture. When it dries, the exteriors of the columns are rock-hard and look like marble. Malcolm Robson, a native of London, England, was commissioned to simulate the original finish with paint. Robson had previously worked in such places as Buckingham Palace, the House of Parliament, and the Athenaeum in Philadelphia. (Arkansas Democrat-Gazette)

Left: Sign hung on the mezzanine balcony, outside, announces the Capital Hotel's reopening. (Arkansas Democrat-Gazette)

Right: In 1983, chef Gary Ketchum was in charge of the kitchen, which produced three meals a day for the eighty-four seat Ashley's Restaurant. A Missourian by birth, Ketchum had worked at prestigious dining establishments throughout the country. He began as an apprentice at the Lodge of the Four Seasons, a resort on the Lake of the Ozarks. He later made stops at the Royal Sonesta and Royal Orleans Hotels in New Orleans, the Mark Hopkins Hotel in San Francisco, and the Pleasant Valley Country Club in Little Rock. He also worked two years for a south Louisiana million-aire who enjoyed Cajun and Creole food. (Arkansas Democrat-Gazette)

Stoermer commands a 140-person staff, including maids, kitchen help, waiters, bartenders, desk clerks and security people.

Stoermer's career was created without college, although for three summers, he attended 10-week sessions at the prestigious Cornell University School of Hotel Administration in Ithaca, N.Y. "I wanted to go to college but I couldn't afford it." However, his Hilton Hotel bosses "shaped and molded me. Hilton is an excellent company. They taught me a lot. I had some very tough taskmasters."

He encourages young people interested in the hotel business to start with a company, such as Hilton, Marriott or Hyatt, that offers a good training program.

"You have to understand people, and then like them. The key is do you understand people."

What you can't learn in the university is the understanding of people, the working with guests," he said. Stoermer has learned that lesson very well.

(*Arkansas Democrat*, October 16, 1988)

His management experience at places like the Waldorf in New York prepared Charles Stoermer, the first general manager of the newly renovated Capital Hotel, for providing for dignitaries and politicians such as Sen. and Mrs. Dan Quayle, Sen. Robert Dole, Michael Dukakis, Jimmy Carter, and Henry Kissinger, all of whom stayed at the Capital. Stoermer had a thank-you note from Vice President George Bush after a 1984 visit, saying "It's a great place to stay." (Arkansas Democrat-Gazette)

Ed Cromwell's dream to save and restore the Capital Hotel was finally realized December 19,1983. The *Democrat* covered the event with a front-page article:

Hotel Reopens Its Doors Today
BY JEFF THATCHER
DEMOCRAT STAFF WRITER

The Capital Hotel—a resurrected Little Rock landmark dating back to 1872—officially opens its doors today. Characterizing the Capital as "a baby learning to take its first step," General Manager Charles Stoermer says the hotel will be prepared for about 90 percent occupancy today with only a few rooms left to be finished.

"We have a small number of rooms at the rate of $49 for a single," Stoermer said. "There are also single rooms priced a $59, $69, and $79, and double rooms priced at $69 and $79. The two-bedroom suites will rent for $250 per night and the one-bedroom suites will rent for $170 per night."

Stoermer said the rates vary because the Capital is trying to attract all kinds of guests. "We are not going to snub anybody," he said. "We want to attract the people of Arkansas when they come to Little Rock. We want them to have the privilege of staying here as much as anyone."

One of the guests who will be staying at the Capital to night is Elizabeth Cassinelli, one of the previous owners. "She will be staying in the Cassinelli Suite," Stoermer said. "I called her a few months ago and told her we had decided to name the suite after her family."

Stoermer, a native of Germany, who previously managed the Waldorf Astoria in New York and some other notable hotels across the country, said that managing the Capital is like a dream come true. "When I was first contacted by Lincoln Hotels (a Dallas-based company that purchased the Capital about a year ago) on May 13, I didn't know what to expect," he said. "But after I took a look at the building the next day, I was so excited that I accepted the offer. I feel very good about being here." Stoermer said that he also fell in love with Little Rock when he first arrived. "When I first came here, I went up to Walton Heights, looked down over the Arkansas River and thought I was in the old country," he said. "I am very confident about this area growing like a lot of other cities."

From a dream kept alive by architect Ed Cromwell, the Capital has ultimately survived to bask in its present glory. For a while, though, the old landmark appeared to be in line for the wrecker's ball.

But after Lincoln Hotels bought the building, a massive reconstruction project was started. The renovation literally rebuilt the Capital from a shell, Stoermer said. "Everybody really pushed, pushed, pushed," he said. "Three months ago, I had the jitters. But as I see the quality of workmanship and craftsmanship with everybody involved, I realize that everybody really knows what they are doing. I am very excited about that, because the hotel was almost totally reconstructed."

As he provided a tour of the Capital's rooms, Stoermer illustrated his enthusiasm for the building and the staff. He seemed to know almost everyone by name. Although the finishing stages were still not complete, instead of harassing the workers, he would gently push them along.

Opposite top: Charles Stoermer instructs the Capital Hotel staff on proper arrangement for room-service settings. (Arkansas Democrat-Gazette)

Opposite bottom: Charles Stoermer, general manager of the Capital Hotel, inspects one of the hotel rooms during the renovation. Prior to becoming the general manager of the capital, Stoermer had had a twenty-seven-year career with Hilton Hotels that eventually led to work at the Plaza and Waldorf Astoria in New York and the Palmer House in Chicago, among others. (Arkansas Democrat-Gazette)

Left: Charles Stoermer, a native of Germany, said that managing the Capital was a dream come true. (Arkansas Democrat-Gazette)

Top left: Local press and business and civic leaders all gathered at the Capital Hotel on December 19, 1983, to celebrate the reopening of the hotel after the two-year renovation and restoration was complete. Then-governor Bill Clinton was present at the ribbon cutting ceremony inside the hotel lobby. (Arkansas Democrat-Gazette)

Top right: Hotel staff gather for a general meeting before the hotel opened for business. (Arkansas Democrat-Gazette)

Bottom: Joe McCarthy *(right)* and Ed Cromwell standing on the mezzanine level on the opening day of the restored hotel. (Arkansas Democrat-Gazette)

In one room waiters and service personnel were practicing serving and taking orders. Their efforts were being videotaped and scrutinized by Victoria International, a training firm that has been working with the Capital staff for two weeks.

"We were able to hire a lot of local talent," Stoermer said. "This is a fine staff composed of a lot of people with good qualities. If we become very successful, we will have a total of 110 employees."

Stoermer emphasized that the Capital will have an intimate atmosphere that will make everyone visiting feel important. "The service area is truly the area that I like to concentrate on," he said. "My sincere hope is that we can be everything that people want us to be."

The Capital will have 123 rooms on its four floors. Additionally, there is a Capital Bar fully furnished with antique furniture and a revolving door; Ashley's Restaurant, which will serve a "recognizable" menu with a touch of Continental cuisine; and Watkins Lounge, a small, intimate bar on the second floor.

Stoermer said he expects the Capital to draw between a 40 percent and 70 percent occupancy rate within the first year of operation. "At this point, I feel that we may not have enough suites," he said. "But it remains to be seen."

Despite the Capital's close proximity to the Excelsior Hotel, Stoermer claims that the two fixtures will be able to work together in a friendly atmosphere.

"The Excelsior and the Capital will have a mutual understanding," he said. "We will be welcome additions to each other. I have a very good relationship with their general manager. We will share both the greatness and the problems."

As he prepared for the opening today, Stoermer admitted that he was looking forward both to the event and 1984.

"I am very excited about the opening," he said. "I know we are prepared. But I really think that next year will be my year." Stoermer hired a prominent chef, Gary Ketchum, to oversee the cuisine. Ketchum, who had previously worked at the Pleasant Valley Country Club, specializes in sculpturing and ice carvings. In 1976, Ketchum was awarded a gold medal for his ice carving in the Pan American Games which were held in New Orleans.

(*Arkansas Democrat,* December 19, 1983)

A final article, which ran in the *Gazette* the day the capital reopened for business, gives us an inside look into Ashley's, the hotel's fine dining establishment:

Restaurant Gives Taste of Elegance

A person doesn't have to stay overnight in the Capital Hotel to experience its elegance and service. The hotel has a gourmet restaurant and a bar, which will be open to the general public, plus several rooms for meetings, luncheons and banquets.

Chef Gary Ketchum is in charge of the kitchen, which will produce three meals a day for the 84-seat Ashley's Restaurant. A Missourian by birth, Ketchum has worked at prestigious dining establishments throughout the country. He began as an apprentice at the Lodge of the Four Seasons, a resort on the Lake of the Ozarks. He later made stops at the Royal Sonesta and Royal Orleans Hotels in New Orleans, the Mark Hopkins Hotel in San Francisco and the Pleasant Valley Country Club in Little Rock. He also worked two years for a southern Louisiana millionaire who enjoyed Cajun and Creole food.

Ketchum said the menu will feature "American Cuisine." It will include some classic continental dishes, some Cajun and Creole cooking and some down-to-earth offerings such as chicken pot pie. It also will feature pates, galantines, wild game and fresh fish—a Ketchum specialty.

"If my seafood purveyor catches a 90-pound shark, we're going to have shark," he said.

There will be fresh endive, kumquats, white asparagus, and grapefruit nearly the size of volleyballs. Some items will have local names such as Stuttgart rice pudding, and Pinnacle Mountain pie.

For the most part, the deluxe menu will command deluxe prices and will be geared to serious diners, but Ketchum said a few items had been included to appeal to people who want to "sample" the Capital's service and fare "and not be put off by an aloofness on the menu."

He said there was "some serious talent in my kitchen." He has worked with all his top assistants before. The Capital is the smallest establishment he has ever worked in, and "here I feel like I've got complete control." He said that was the reason he took the job rather than one with a large hotel or restaurant.

"I don't want to walk around with a clipboard in my hand and die behind the range with a bottle of Chivas in my hand like a lot of chefs," he said.

The restaurant where Ketchum's food will be served is under the direction of Maitre d' Michel Lemy. The restaurant is in the northeast corner of the building and borders Markham Street and the lobby.

The roomy Capital Bar is off the lobby in the northwest corner of the building. A revolving door provides an entrance at Markham and Louisiana Streets and the building's windows provide a good view of the street and sidewalk traffic and the Excelsior across the street.

There are five private meeting rooms on the first and second floors. They will seat between 35 and 90 persons for private dinners. The rooms have lots of wood molding and detail work to give them an air of formality.

The rooms carry historic names such as Quapaw, De Soto, and Cherokee. One room on the second floor is called the Brooks Parlor. Across the hall is the Baxter Parlor. They commemorate the Brooks-Baxter war, a political struggle for the statehouse that was played out across the street in 1873 and 1874.

The Watkins Lounge on the second floor was named for an early owner of the hotel. The lounge also can be used for a dinner for up to 150 persons. The lounge adjoins the Markham Street balcony, which can be used for a reception of up to 100 persons.

(*Arkansas Gazette,* December 19, 1983)

United States Senate
Washington, D. C.

12-27-83

Ed

Just a note to say sincere
congratulations upon "The Great Achievement" —
a the "miracle of Markham Street".

This great hotel would have become
a Parking lot (or something else awful) had
it not been for your vision, caring and
persistence.

Also, let me thank you for the
nice words about me at your press conference.
you were most generous.

wishing you and your venture the
greatest success —

David

December 27, 1983, note
from then-senator David
Pryor to Ed Cromwell,
congratulating him on
the reopening of the
Capital Hotel. Pryor
played an important
role in saving an
Economic Development
Administration loan that
was part of the finance
package to fund the
restoration of the
Capital. *(From Ed
Cromwell's personal files)*

STATE OF ARKANSAS
BILL CLINTON
GOVERNOR

December 22, 1988

Ed Cromwell
One Spring Street
Little Rock, AR 72201

Dear Ed:

It is a great honor for all Arkansans that the restoration of the Capital Hotel was selected as one of the nation's most outstanding preservation projects. I congratulate you for your participation in the restoration of this fine hotel. I know it was very exciting for you to receive the award from Secretary of Interior Donald Hodel.

The Capital Hotel stands as one of Little Rock's finest hotels and as a beautiful reminder of our state's proud heritage. Thanks to your professional ability and that of other Arkansans involved in the restoration we can all enjoy the excellent fruits of your efforts--a beautifully restored Capital Hotel with the charm and elegance it originally had.

Best wishes for continued success.

Sincerely,

Bill Clinton

BC:cf

Personal note from then-governor Bill Clinton to Ed Cromwell, congratulating him on the National Historic Preservation award given to the Capital Hotel under Ronald Reagan. *(From Ed Cromwell's personal files)*

3-8-84

Dear Mr. Cromwell —

I may never go to the south of France, or Rome or London, but these tired old eyes have been dazzled by the restoration of The Capital Hotel — the place is a Palace!

I want to thank you for your vision, for the impeccable manner in which the restoration was executed and for the sense of pride I feel in our city that a landmark of this magnificence was spared the wrecking ball. By comparison, The Excelsior is diminished!

I will be retiring this May and wondered what grand place I might go for a brief vacation. Now, I don't even have to leave the city limits. With my friends I may enjoy libation in the warm & wonderful old Bar, dinner in the elegant Ashley restaurant, take a leisurely stroll through the columned lobby, up to the mezzanine and out on the balcony then for the ride of my life on certainly the roomiest elevator in the South!

The Capital Hotel — what a treasure, what an exquisite example of genuine taste, pure 24K class and old world charm. Isn't it beautiful? Isn't it a work of art?

Sincerely,
Marjorie Barkley

Personal letter from Little Rock resident Marjorie Barkley, congratulating Ed Cromwell on the renovation of the Capital Hotel. Cromwell received many such letters from local residents "dazzled" by Cromwell's accomplishment. *(From Ed Cromwell's personal files)*

CHAPTER FOUR

THE NEW CAPITAL HOTEL

Restoring the Capital Hotel turned out to be an easier job than turning a profit. Despite all the fanfare and publicity, the hotel suffered from low occupancy (below 50 percent) and room rates (fifty-five dollars daily). There was no question that the Capital was now the Ritz of Little Rock, but as a business venture it was soon in financial jeopardy.

From 1983 to 1986 the Lincoln Hotel Group struggled to make payments. On the verge of bankruptcy, Jack Stephens took an interest in the hotel and appointed Scott Ford (now CEO and president of Alltel) to buy the Capital.

Ford went to work for Warren Stephens in the Corporate Finance Department of Stephens, Inc. Eventually he spent more and more time working directly for Jack Stephens. In 1988 Scott went to work full time for the elder Stephens and continued to work there until 1996 when he left the investment banking firm to join the Alltel management team. "I was still working in the Corporate Financing Department," says Ford, "and it was the first assignment Jack gave me. He called me up one day and said, 'I want to buy the Capital Hotel.' I think that he heard that it was a nice place and that it was in financial straits. And he said, 'I want you to buy it for me.' And I said 'Well, okay.' This was in 1986."

Ford immediately hired the Rose Law Firm who assigned a young associate named Bert Biguet (pronounced bu-GAY) to the project. Ford describes Biguet, from Fort Smith, as having "a mind like a lint brush,"—a valuable asset in business negotiations. With Biguet by his side, Ford approached Ed Mace at the Lincoln Hotel Group. "They didn't want to give up equity, but they wanted a loan. Of course we said no."

After some haggling, Lincoln finally conceded and gave Stephens a 25 percent equity ownership in the hotel in exchange for a $250,000 loan. "Then they couldn't pay that loan back," says Ford. " So, we made another loan. All the while, the only people that were making any money, was the hotel management company. They were charging 4 percent of gross, or about 20 percent of the net cash flow."

The money that was being made was being pocketed by Lincoln to the tune of about $400,000 a year. This left little money to pay off the bond debt and pay basic operating expenses. Lincoln was experiencing financial difficulties with its other properties; they suggested that another hotel management group like Omni be brought in to run the Capital. "We said no," says Ford, "because we wanted to run it as an independent hotel and because the hotel couldn't afford a four hundred grand a year in hotel management service fees. So anyway . . . we're down in a conference room in Texas and they're saying, 'Well we're seventy-five and you're twenty-five and by gosh that's what we're doing.' We told them you know you're under

Arkansas law and in Arkansas a partnership is a partner and a partner gets a vote and we vote N-O. Of course, he didn't know that it wasn't a credible legal argument. But this move slowed things down long enough for them to miss another payment and we bought some more of the hotel."

The Lincoln empire was collapsing in 1987 and 1988, and Stephens stepped in and amidst legal maneuvering and negotiations eventually picked up ownership of the hotel. Ford narrates the chain of events . . .

We weren't really clear on how or if we were going to structure a deal. But we knew that if we bought it and took control, we would put enough money in it where it would be solvent. About that time, they [Lincoln] defaulted on the EDA debt and the Metro Center Improvement Bonds.

So these first mortgage bonds were not trading anywhere. We called the trustee and asked them if they would sell them. They held an auction and we showed up along with the Mass Financial Junk Bond Unit and somebody else. I called Ernie Butler and asked him what should we bid? He said, "Never bid an even number. What do you think they're worth?" We said, "About 80 cents on the dollar." Then he said, "Then I would bid .82175." So we bid .82175 and Mass Financial Bid .82. So then Mass Financial sued us for nothing. Then they called back and said that they would settle if we would sell them half the bonds. We said you're suing us for nothing; you're the one that didn't turn in your bidding on time, hit the road. They dropped the suit, and we bought the bonds.

We ended up closing up the equity deal and buying the hotel. This is around 1988 or 1989. So, we put our equity in the hotel, shored up the hotel, then we sold the bonds. I think we bought them at 82 and sold them 119. It was still a good deal for the buyer. We made as much money selling the bonds as we had invested. We basically owned the hotel for free! That was effective. We got the occupancy up to 55 or 60 percent, and then we sold the bonds and made a profit . . . You know because now the hotel was solid 'cause we could put up whatever equity had to be put up to keep them afloat, we were going to pay them off. People recognized that.

Of course there were weeks and months between all these events . . . By the time we finished it took us a couple of years, several lawsuits, threatened bankruptcy, bonds from another lawsuit; it took us two years to get the hotel. But when we got it, we basically owned it for free. Having Stephens involved with the hotel increased the perceived value of the Capital Hotel property. We were able to get the room rates up. The average daily room rate spread over what the Excelsior was getting, just shot up like a hockey stick; occupancy went up. In the middle of the transition, Stoermer just up and left; Lincoln went bankrupt and that was that. We owned the hotel 100 percent.

The President's Historic Preservation Award

In the middle of the financial controversy, the Capital Hotel was awarded the National Historic Preservation Award under Ronald Reagan. A press release dated November 18, 1988, from the office of the Advisory Council on Historic Preservation reads,

The Capital Hotel will receive a National Historic Preservation Award on November 18, 1988 at ceremonies in Washington. Only 18 outstanding preservation projects and programs have been selected for the award, which recognizes excellence in federally assisted historic preservation. Edwin B. Cromwell, the project's architect and investor, will accept the award which will be presented by Advisory Council on Historic Preservation Chairman F. W. Rogers and Secretary of the Interior Donald P. Hodel.

During this time of financial maneuvering between Stephens and Lincoln, the *Democrat* ran a huge, front-page article in the business section heaping accolades on Stoermer (October 16, 1988). The article began, "Humble start leads manager to luxury of Capital":

The Capital was managed by the Dallas-based Lincoln Hotel Corp. until that firm went out of business about a year ago. In November [1987] Stephens Inc., a Little Rock investment firm, purchased a one-third interest in the hotel, Stoermer said. "I'm now reporting to the Stephens family." Monetary Investment of New York, which represents a group of New York investors, owns the remaining two-thirds share, Stoermer noted. "It would be nice if Stephens bought the entire hotel." Stoermer said.

And then later in the article:

The revived hotel has also turned into a success. Stoermer said the hotel is performing "better and better" from year to year.

Within months after the article was published, Stoermer left. Joe Rantisi, the current general manager of the Capital remembers a call from the former general manager. "He [Stoermer] called me up in 1989 and said 'I am leaving the Capital Hotel,' and he wanted me to be the hotel manager. I said 'Charlie no, I just moved here to Tennessee . . . But I have a friend who is looking for a job. I know him very well. I will recommend him.'"

That "friend" was Jim Fayek who had worked with Rantisi at the Waldorf in New York. Fayek worked at the Waldorf for a number of years and his last position there was as Towers Manager. Joe Rantisi said, "Jim came down a couple of times for an interview and met with the Stephens people and their partners and he was hired."

While Scott Ford handled the bulk of the business negotiations, Rick Turner represented the Stephens' management interest and hired Fayek who was successful in managing the hotel back to a more stable financial status.

Fayek and Rantisi would continue to talk at least once a week; their friendship lasted twenty-one years. "Back in 1994, I found out that he [Fayek] was very sick," recounts Rantisi. "I came to visit him. In '94, I had not seen him for seven years, I came to see him and when he talked to me, he said, 'I know I am going to die.' Here is a guy who knew he had terminal cancer, who had no chances of recovery and had the decency enough to hire someone to replace himself. He kept the position with the hotel until he passed away. It was a bad sickness—cancer—it was only three months from when he was diagnosed until he passed away. I came to the funeral and that was when I met Rick Turner for the first time."

Joe Rantisi's Rising Career

Joe Rantisi was born in Palestine in 1947. His parents were refugees after the Arab-Israeli War, and the family lived in Jordan. "My mother was a school headmistress and my father was a metallurgist," recalls Rantisi. "I went to a private school. My parents felt that they needed me to a have a better education. They both sacrificed a lot for my brother and myself to have the best education. We all had to work much harder than anyone else to establish ourselves, and I think that was ingrained in me—traditional family values and a strong work ethic."

Rantisi was a good student and at one time seriously considered medical school. Eventually he entered a three-year, executive hotel management program in Madrid. "I went to my parents and told them about the program. They couldn't understand the concept, 'You want to be a waiter?' This was in 1964, 1965. I told them that is what I want to do and I had made the commitment. My father passed away in 1966, one year after I went into the program. So, I had to leave the college early, went back home to help with the family business."

Rantisi's mother eventually sold the family business and helped to pay for her son's second year of college. "While there in the West Bank, Jordan, I had an internship at the Mount Scopus Hotel in Jerusalem. I returned to complete my second year of college, but I was advised that the program had been cancelled. I made a deal with the college to allow me to complete the program under the old structure since I had already spent one year, and if I did not pass the final test for graduation, I would then join the new program. I did both the second and third year in one year, and I did pass and graduated in 1967. It was a tough year because I spent all my time studying and graduated second in my class."

Upon graduation Rantisi was caught in the political crisis of the June 6, 1967, war in the Middle East and essentially became a fugitive for several years, unable to return to his home. "I managed to reach England after three months of attempts, and I got deported and jailed on the first one. From there I traveled to the Bahamas and managed to stay there without a visa for four years."

Eventually Joe Rantisi was able to make his way to New York, attracted by the hope of work and a new beginning.

A New World

"I had survived. I got to New York with my green card and started looking for a job." Rantisi set his sights high and approached the Waldorf which had advertised a position for coffee shop manager. Rantisi interviewed for the position, was offered the job, but turned it down! "The guy who interviewed me was absolutely flabbergasted. He looked at me and said, 'You just practically got off the boat. You got a job in management as the coffee shop manager and you're turning it down? What is the problem?' I told him the job included Saturdays and Sundays. I had just gotten married and I would never see my wife. I will find a job somewhere else. He was mad when I left."

In spite of this inauspicious beginning, Rantisi was later offered a position as assistant floor manager of the Waldorf Astoria—one of new York's finest hotels.

Joseph B. Rantisi

"I worked harder than most people, at the expense of my marriage and my family." But the work paid off, and Rantisi was made executive assistant and then manager.

It was at the Waldorf that Rantisi first met Charles Stoermer. Stoermer was the maitre d' of the Marco Polo Club, a private club in the hotel. "I didn't have much contact with him: the hotel had 2200 employees. So, we didn't spend much time together. I knew of him and he knew of me. It was like living in the same town but not getting to know each other."

After eight successful years at the Waldorf, Rantisi was ready for a change. In 1981 he accepted a position with the Washington Hilton. Stoermer had also previously made the move from the Waldorf to the Hilton.

> When I transferred to the Washington Hilton as the resident manager, Charles Stoermer was already in management; Charlie's ambition was to become general manager. September of 1981 is when I went to the Washington Hilton, and I worked with Charlie for over a year and a half. It was in April of 1983 when I got a call back from the Waldorf again. The guy who hired me was now the manager for the Waldorf and senior vice president. He wanted me to come back to work with them. So I went back at the Waldorf as vice president/ manager, and it was quite a great honor in the business, one of the highest, you know, to work there and learn how to run the business, and I enjoyed it very much.
>
> Over the years I have been personally honored to have met every president since I came to this country. I met Nixon after he left the White House. President Clinton did the ribbon cutting at the Capital Hotel. I've met Nancy Reagan, Ronald Reagan, and Vice President Bush. I met President Mubarak, Idi Amin, the Dalai Lama, Golda Meir, King Hussein of Jordan. Actually in 1980, King Hussein offered me a position with him in Jordan,

but my family was not ready to move back to the Middle East. You meet so many people in this business and you have such an opportunity to learn many valuable things from them. It has been an extraordinary experience.

The Capital Hotel

In 1994, after the death of Jim Fayek, Rick Turner interviewed and hired Rantisi to run the hotel on behalf of Jack Stephens.

"I started March 21, 1994, at the Capital. The Capital had been open since the December of 1983. They had only had two general managers since it opened, and I knew both of them. They were a very important part of my life, Charlie Stoermer and Jim Fayek. The hardest thing for me was to come to this place and to take over where Jim left off. If he had left the job, it would have been easier; but he had passed away. He loved this hotel; he loved the people. He had remarried, had a new family; it was very hard for me to do that. He wanted tradition; he learned a lot at the Waldorf."

The Setting of a Tone

"You know, we're still formal here," said Joe Rantisi who sat for my interview still wearing his suit coat. "When people come to the Capital Hotel, they expect tradition; they expect the highest professional appearances. We are still holding on to a tradition that no one else does. We have a responsibility at the Capital Hotel, to do something and give something to Arkansas that is for Arkansas alone. It would be a betrayal to the people if we did not do so."

Rantisi is quick to give credit to the success of the Capital to the Stephens family. "Mr. Stephens saw the long-range picture. The Stephens look down the road. They don't look at today or tomorrow, they look down the road. They saw a potential in this operation even when it wasn't doing well."

Rantisi's Tour of the Capital Hotel

During an interview with Joe Rantisi, I asked him to take me on a "virtual tour" and describe to me what a guest would see and experience upon arrival at the Capital Hotel. Joe started right at the front door:

> If you were a guest, I would start in the lobby and meet you at the front door. The minute you walk into the hotel, it is like stepping back in time. Everything is beautiful: the marble walls and terrazzo floors, the faux marble columns. Then we would walk into the lobby and look at the furnishings and see that it is from a different era; you don't find this in the south. Everything looks pristine, nice, in place and right; that is the way I want it. I have been taught in this business that first impressions are very important.
>
> You really can't say "Today we have a VIP guest, let's spruce up." Here we are always ready to go because we never know who is going to walk through the door and who will want to do business with us.
>
> Probably about fifty or sixty thousand people come through the Capital Hotel a year—each one of them is a customer or prospective customer.

The Capital Hotel front
entrance after the reopening.
(Photograph by Peter Paige)

Joe Rantisi, the Capital's general manager, describes the experience of walking through the hotel's front door as "stepping back in time. Everything is beautiful: the marble walls and terrazzo floors the faux marble columns . . . you can see that it is from a different era . . . Everything looks pristine, nice, in place and right; that is the way I want it."
(Cromwell Architects and Engineers, Inc.)

Hotel Lobby looking from the front door towards the grand staircase and up to the mezzanine. Joe Rantisi says that the hotel takes its guests "back into a different century . . . here you could be in the Plaza or the Waldorf." *(Cromwell Architects and Engineers, Inc.)*

We turn down a lot of business because it is too big for us; we don't have enough space. We have to just take the business that we can accommodate. Our philosophy that I learned a long time ago is if you really can't satisfy a customer, and you know that up front, then don't take the chance of trying to do business with them, because you are committing suicide as well as saying to the customer, "Your needs are a lot more than I can handle, and I do not want you to be unhappy because I would like to have your business."

From the lobby I would take you up the grand stairs and up to the mezzanine. Again note the arches, columns, stained glass windows, the skylight. This is a different kind of hotel, it's a charming little place.

Then we would take you to the guest rooms or to a meeting room; you'll see fine furnishings, lighting, even the wallpaper will take you back into a different century. You could be in the Plaza or the Waldorf—that is exactly what we wanted to achieve. Unless you look out the window, you wouldn't

Hotel lobby as it appeared in 2001 under the general management of Joe Rantisi and the Stephens family. *(Photo by Janet Warlick, Camera Work)*

know you are in Little Rock. When you walk into the room, you could be in one of the best hotels in the country or the world because everything is done in style.

We have 126 hotel rooms, 5 of them are suites—they have a bedroom and a living room. When people come into the hotel, they kind of jump back because they all have names like the Grant or the Cassinelli and the Auten. This is better than just reading the numbers. People walking in don't expect that quality in Little Rock. We design them with the people who have the best homes in the United States in mind.

One of the beautiful things about this hotel is its high ceilings. We have three hotel levels for guest rooms. You have a fourteen-foot ceiling on the second floor and a twelve-foot ceiling on the third floor, and then you have ten-and-a-half-foot ceilings on the fourth floor. Our rooms are relatively small, but because of the ceiling height they feel grand. We have ten- to twelve-foot windows in the rooms.

Looking down the grand staircase from the upper floors of the Capital Hotel. Throughout the hotel there is an openness to the both the public places and private rooms. There are fourteen-foot ceilings on the second floor, and twelve-foot ceilings on the third floor, and ten-and-a-half foot ceilings on the fourth floor. *(Cromwell Architects and Engineers, Inc.)*

The Capital Hotel has 126 hotel rooms, 5 of them are suites. There are also a number of private dining and meeting rooms. The mezzanine, shown here, continues to offer a comfortable yet elegant place for parties and for guests to visit. *(Photograph by Peter Paige)*

Interior Renovation, 1996–2001

The initial restoration that was done by Cromwell and the Lincoln Hotel group had been completed on a tight budget. Most of the money had gone into the structural foundation and public places, leaving the actual guest rooms at par, but not above par in terms of comfort and elegance. Having worked at the Waldorf, Rantisi had a vision of what the Capital might be: a hotel with the quality and luxury of a Four Seasons or Plaza. He and his staff put together a five-year plan. The Stephens approved the plan and a major internal renovation and upgrading of the hotel began in 1996. Paula Dixon, a well-known residential interior designer from Charlotte, North Carolina, and Warren Stephens' sister-in-law, was hired to help with the renovation. Dixon's influence added southern charm and hospitality to Rantisi's hotel management experience. The result was that the guest rooms had all the comforts of home in a commercial environment. Rantisi's attention to minute detail included such things as phone and electrical jacks placed at strategic, functional places in guest rooms, upgraded fire and safety devices, and luxury bedding. Things such as the

Another view of the current mezzanine where music is frequently provided for special parties and receptions. *(Photo by Janet Warlick, Camera Work)*

replacement of windows (there were twelve different styles of windows in the Capital) had to be approved by the National Historic Trust.

Starting about 1996 we took everything apart. We started from scratch with brand new carpet, wallpaper, draperies, a new telephone system with data ports. We did a whole lot of things that hotels that charge four or five hundred dollars a night for rooms have, and here in Little Rock, for a little bit over a hundred dollars, you get the same features and quality service to boot, and we are proud of that.

(Photograph by Peter Paige)

(Photograph by Peter Paige)

(Photograph by Peter Paige)

(Photo by Janet Warlick, Camera Work)

Opposite and this page: Further upgrading and interior renovation of the Capital began in 1996. Paula Dixon, a well-known, residential interior designer from Charlotte, North Carolina, was hired to help with the renovation. Attention to minute details included such things as phone and electrical jacks placed at strategic, functional places in guest rooms, upgraded fire and safety devices, and luxury bedding.

The Capital Hotel Staff

Aside from the physical attributes of the hotel, Rantisi emphasized again and again the importance of a dedicated staff willing to pitch in to do whatever it takes to make their guests feel at home.

I am proud of the people that we have because they are what make this building, this hotel, as beautiful it is. If it were not for the people working here, it wouldn't survive. It's great to have the right kind of people working with us to make it happen. That is what makes a hotel, people. We have the winningest combination in the world, we have a good product, good people.

A lot of people who work for the hotel business are used to the large corporate environment, where a person has a domain, a specific job description. Things here at the Capital are different. For example, food and beverage people are not just food and beverage people here. I do 90 percent of the interviewing and hiring. We don't hire someone for just one position. They understand that their job is on a larger scope, encompassing other things besides their immediate job. We never know what the customer might need, so we anticipate by preparing the staff. Everyone here works for the guest, and they have a primary job and secondary responsibilities—whatever it takes to take care of the customers. We try to select the right kind of people who can offer excellent customer service under pressure in a hotel environment.

In our hotel we have hundreds of people coming in and out a day. Every position in this hotel is important to the satisfaction of the guests. Even the position of housekeeper in our hotel is extremely important. They don't get a lot of credit in other hotels for the work that they do. A housekeeper is someone who keeps track of your home, and our staff takes pride in what they do. I had a gentleman from a major network in Little Rock walk into my office one day, just last week. He was staying here because he was in the process of purchasing a house, and he walked into my office with an envelope with cash in it, a whole bunch of hundred-dollar bills. I thought he wanted to buy something, but he wanted to tell me that he had left it in his room that morning. Housekeeping came in to clean it after he left, and when he returned, the envelope was still there with every dollar, exactly in the same place. He just wanted me to know that. I was not surprised that the money was found as he had left it.

Ashley's Fine Dining

Ashley's has long been known for its white-table-cloth dining: a variety of gourmet menu items served in an elegant atmosphere. Here Mr. Rantisi give us some insights and history of this award-winning restaurant at the Capital Hotel:

The restaurant opened in December of 1983; it introduced fine dining to Little Rock. We introduced table-side service and the best dining the city had to offer. From its opening, the restaurant has always been full. Now, in the past ten or fifteen years, you have had other fine dining restaurants open as well, including Alouette's, Josephine's, and others. They have not been able to compete with Ashley's because we set the standard in good times and bad. Ashley's has been able to remain consistent.

(Photograph by Peter Paige)

Ashley's Restaurant opened in December of 1983 and helped introduce fine dining to Little Rock.

(Photo by Janet Warlick, Camera Work)

More restaurants these days have become more casual, and many more chain restaurants are popping up everywhere. But people still want a place to go that is fine and unique. The restaurant has kept the same menu, for the most part, over the years. We have modified the bar to include more after-work professionals; we want them to come down to the hotel for drinks and possibly dinner.

We started to get feedback from our customers and business travelers and started to modify the menu to include lighter, more health-conscious dishes as well as retaining some of the full, heavier sorts of meals that some of our guests enjoy. We shut down for three weeks and renovated the entire restaurant and menu based on the suggestions of our diners and guests. Those suggestions have brought us one of the best wine lists in the country. The award-winning menu at Ashley's is updated twice a year. We are constantly seeking out and testing new items.

A Unique Wine Cellar

Situated off the hotel kitchen (you have to walk through the kitchen to get to it) is a new—yet seemingly old—wine cellar. With its unique blend of rich woods and exposed brick, the new wine cellar has a simple, yet very elegant atmosphere about it. Joe Rantisi proudly discoursed on the concept behind this new addition to the Capital Hotel:

Originally we wanted to have a wine cooler and storage. Warren Stephens wanted that as well, but he took the project well beyond our original concept. He wanted something equal to the 21 Club, a one-of-a-kind place. He wanted to put in a beautiful table in the wine cellar so people who wanted to have an even more unique dining experience could have a fabulous meal among very wonderful wines. The way you get down there is through the back, often closed-off-to-the-public area of the hotel. I don't think anyone in the area would have come up with as unique and wonderful a concept as this.

We have over three thousand bottles of wines, many very rare. This special dining has the best there is to offer, from flatware, to audio-visual equipment. Everything in the room is Arkansas made . . . the ironwork was done in Fayetteville, Tommy Farrell did the custom design on the table. Bob East and his construction crew at East Harding did a fabulous job. The Cromwell firm did the design, and they were extremely creative in how they made the place totally modern in terms of equipment and conveniences, yet it looks like a part of the original hotel.

The Capital Bar

Walk into the Capital Bar at lunchtime on a weekday, and you'll see a mix of business and civic leaders, politicians, lawyers, and judges. It is a high-powered mix of patrons that has made the Capital Bar a legend.

"Some people said that the rules were made at the statehouse," says Rantisi, "but the laws were made at the Capital Bar. It has a rich political history because of its location across from the Old State House. More recently, when Clinton was running for

Situated off the hotel kitchen (you have to walk through the kitchen to get to it) is a new—yet seemingly old—wine cellar with over three thousand bottles of wine. The cellar was completed in 2001. *(Photo by Janet Warlick, Camera Work)*

(Photo by Janet Warlick, Camera Work)

president, many people who were in Little Rock were writing stories on this southern governor. They discovered the Capital Hotel and loved it. The bar was a meeting place for the who's who of the national press. It was incredible."

Accolades and Awards

As I sat in Joe Rantisi's office, the general manager paused and pulled a file from his desk. He opened the file to display dozens of news clips, reviews, and articles praising the Capital Hotel:

> We have won almost every major hotel award there is, from Condé Nast Travel Magazine to AAA Four Diamond Award—we were the only hotel in Arkansas to have won that. We have won the *Arkansas Times* Best Hotel, Best Restaurant since 1996; from the *Democrat-Gazette,* we won best hotel, and Ashley's won best restaurant, the most romantic restaurant. Every time we win an award, we tell the staff that we can't let it go to our head, we have to stay focused. We work hard for the customers, not for the awards. If we work hard for the customers, the awards will come to us. We have been nominated for the Wine Spectator Award and Wine Cellar Award.

(Photograph by Peter Paige)

Some people have called us the little Waldorf. I take that as a compliment and the Waldorf should as well. It speaks very highly of both hotels. In today's environment, to be able to have that type of quality service means a lot, and we have a responsibility to the people of Little Rock to keep it right.

Opposite and this page: Interior shot of the Capital Bar, long the meeting place for politicians and business leaders. The Capital Bar was host to the dozens of national media reporters and political analysts during Clinton's first presidential campaign in the early '90s.

A Closing Note: Thank you, Mr. Stephens

And so we come full circle with our story of the Capital Hotel—from 1872 when William P. Denckla first conceived the original building that housed a variety of retail shops and professional offices, to the "Little Waldorf" described by general manager Joe Rantisi, and now owned by Jack Stephens. For Denckla, the motivating factor was simply an economic one, but as Rantisi explains, there is much more than a monetary interest behind Jack Stephens's fondness for the property:

One time during Clinton's first presidential election, a major national network reporter was trying to phone out of the hotel, but because of the telephone traffic was unable to place the call. He took me aside and yelled at me for the phone problems, and I kept telling him that because of the campaign and the great influx of reporters, visitors, and media that all the phones in the area were jammed. Jack Stephens overheard all this, and he walked up to the reporter and said, "Mr. So and So, my name is Jack Stephens. Can I buy you a drink?" So the two of them went to the bar, and the guy came back later to the desk and said, "I am sorry. I was upset with the phone system, and I took it out on you."

Whether people in this hotel spend one dollar or a thousand, Mr. Stephens has always been very nice and gracious to each and every person and appreciates them. This hotel is but a very small part of the Stephens' entire investments, but they make the time that is needed to keep this the top hotel.

I have been around the hotel business for just about thirty years, and I love it. I tell our employees, as good as you are professionally, your attitude will show through if you do not like your job. People are not stupid; they can tell when you genuinely enjoy it or are faking it.

If it wasn't for the Stephens family, this hotel would be a dilapidated old building. But because of their faith in the people of this state, they have turned it into a living piece of history for everyone to enjoy.